Rum & Red Peppers

80 CARIBBEAN, ARMENIAN, MIDDLE EASTERN & MEDITERRANEAN RECIPES

WAYNE GERARD TROTMAN & SHERRIE TROTMAN
PHOTOGRAPHS & DESIGN BY WAYNE GERARD TROTMAN

RED MOON

www.redmoon.co.uk

RUM & RED PEPPERS
80 CARIBBEAN, ARMENIAN, MIDDLE EASTERN & MEDITERRANEAN RECIPES
BY WAYNE GERARD TROTMAN & SHERRIE TROTMAN

This First Edition published in 2016 by Red Moon Productions Ltd. Surrey, UK.

ISBN 978-0-9567872-6-2

www.waynegerardtrotman.com

"There is no love sincerer than the love of food."
— George Bernard Shaw

CONTENTS

INTRODUCTION

Cooking is about love and sharing. Parents love to feed their children, just as a lover delights in placing delicious morsels between the lips of her beloved. Out of necessity, we may cook only for ourselves but cooking for others is one of life's greatest pleasures. Cooking evokes a sense of nostalgia - treasured childhood memories, special occasions, jovial family gatherings, intimate relationships and timeless places. Mother, father, grandmother, grandfather, favourite aunt or uncle- we each have that special person or handful of people whose culinary creations helped shape our lives. Cooking honours those we love and binds us to our communities.

While embarking on this adventure, a few basic rules should be adhered to. Hygiene is of utmost importance. Ingredients such as vegetables, meat, fish and poultry, should be washed with cool, running water. Utensils must be clean- preferably washed in hot, soapy water or using an automatic dishwasher. Items washed in hot, soapy water should be thoroughly rinsed in very hot water and left to dry on a rack. Avoid using cloths for drying. Storage containers should be sterilised prior to use and either airtight or hermetically sealed. Always follow the manufacturer instructions for equipment and ingredients. Heed recommended storage times and, where possible, note the date items are stored.

Please refer to the condiments section, where you will find recipes for our 'secret' ingredients such as Green Seasoning, Hot Pepper Sauce, Red Pepper Paste and Trinidadian Burnt Sugar Syrup, all essential for recreating the authentic flavours of traditional recipes. As a vital ingredient, a few of our newly-created recipes also use Rum & Red Peppers, which can be found in the drinks section.

The Republic of Trinidad and Tobago is a wealthy, two-island Caribbean nation, situated near the northern edge of the South American mainland, inhabited primarily by people of African and Indian descent.

Trinidad and Tobago has one of the most diverse cuisines in the world, blending African, Creole, Cajun, Indian, South Asian, Amerindian, English, French, Portuguese, Spanish, Latin American, Chinese, Jewish, and Arabic influences.

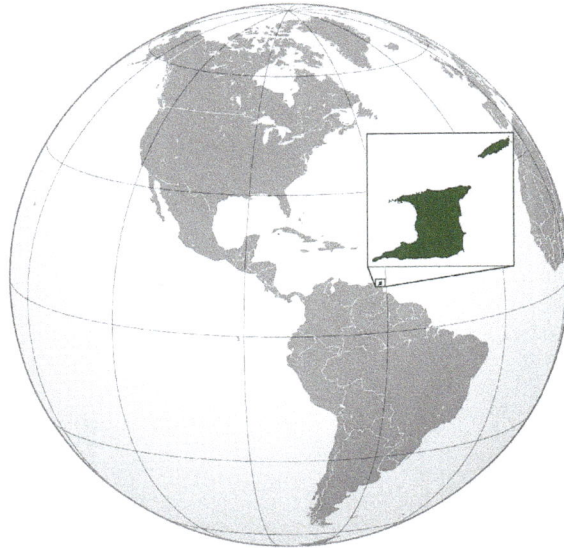

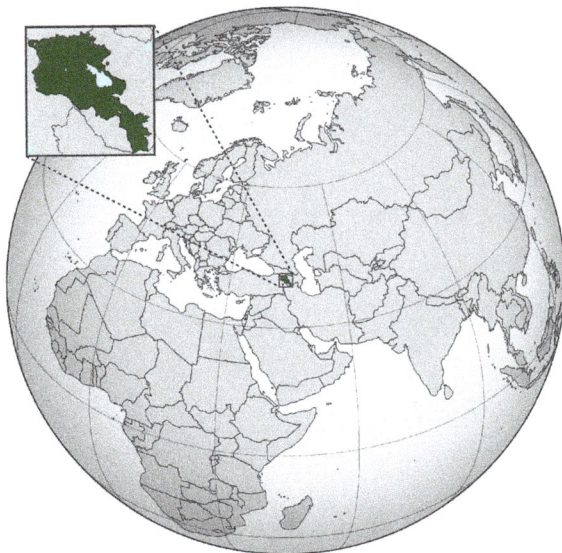

Bounded by Georgia, Azerbaijan, Iran and Turkey, and constituting only one-tenth of historical Armenia, the Republic of Armenia is a sovereign state in the South Caucasus region of Eurasia. Armenia was the first state in the world to adopt Christianity as its official religion.

Armenian cuisine reflects the history, geographical location, and traditional crops and animals of the Armenian people and diaspora, while also incorporating outside influences.

OUR RECIPES

Rum & Red Peppers features simple recipes that reflect the traditional cuisines and rich cultural diversity of Trinidad and Tobago, the Caribbean, Armenia, the Middle East and the Mediterranean. As much as possible, our interpretations call for readily available ingredients, identified by British, Trinidadian, and Armenian names. Some ingredients are known by a myriad of local and cultural names and it would not be feasible to list them all.

Our recipes are of three types- traditional, inspired, and brand new creations. Traditional recipes include Caribbean Chicken Stew, Callaloo, Rice & Peas, Sorrel, Black Cake, Lamb & White Bean Stew, Dolma, Lahmajoon, Boreg, Tabouleh and Vospov Kufteh. Inspired recipes are our variations of popular drinks and dishes including Cuba Roja, Wayne's Mai Tai, Wayne's Piña Colada, Peppermint Milo, Christmas Crackers and Meatballs in Rum Sauce. Finally, we are particularly proud of our new creations, which include Rum & Red Peppers Chicken, Grilled Mango Chicken, Caribbean Sea Bream, Salsa Salmon, Boozy Fruit Cupcakes, Almond Berry Cake, Sorrel Sorbet, Black Rock, Fiery Passion and Spartan.

In the traditional cultures of Trinidad and Tobago and Armenia, cookbooks are seldom more than reference material. Recipes are handed down from one generation to another and often rendered by experienced individuals accustomed to cooking instinctively, by sight, taste and scent. Measurements are drawn from experience, not from exact cup sizes, clearly defined measuring jugs or precise scales. Be that as it may, our recipes were designed to be used by anyone capable of cooking, regardless of their skill level. Therefore, we have included fairly precise measurements and, in some cases, information regarding the ingredients we prefer.

Our recipes also reflect our increasingly busy lifestyles; and, as such, some incorporate modern, time-saving, mechanical marvels such as bread makers and ice-cream makers, as well as ready-made ingredients such as pastry sheets, tortilla wraps, fruit juices, tinned callaloo and coconut milk. Several recipes call for dark or white rum. We prefer Trinidadian or Cuban rums. However, any good quality, well-refined rums can be used. Angostura bitters, however, has no substitute.

We hope that you will enjoy our easy-to-follow recipes and employ them in the spirit of discovery and adventure with which they were written. Be bold, and use the note pages to chronicle your own tastes, preferences, and variations. But, most of all, have fun.

COLOUR CODES

We've arranged the recipes that we cook and enjoy at home into three broad categories: **Armenian & Middle Eastern** food inspired by Armenian cuisine or popular within Armenian communities. **Caribbean** food mainly inspired by the diverse cuisine of Trinidad & Tobago. **Mediterranean** foods for which we have developed new recipes and unique variations that compliment our dishes.

Armenian & Middle Eastern

Caribbean

Mediterranean

OVEN TEMPERATURES

Here in the UK, we use celsius, also known as centigrade (°C) or gas marks for our oven heat settings. For convenience we have rounded our Fahrenheit (°F) temperature conversions to the nearest 10.

Gas Mark	°C	°F	Description
1	140	280	very cool
2	150	300	cool
3	160	320	warm
4	180	360	moderate
5	190	370	} fairly hot
6	200	390	
7	210	410	hot
8	220	430	} very hot
9	240	470	

Condiments

GREEN SEASONING

Most households in Trinidad and Tobago have a recipe for green seasoning handed down from one generation to another. This is our variation, which adds a distinctive flavour to our recipes. It is simple to make and really adds a new dimension to food.

50g/1¾oz thyme (finely chopped)
50g/1¾oz oregano (finely chopped)
3 bell peppers - red, green, or yellow (finely chopped)
4 large white onions (finely chopped)
5 cloves garlic (crushed)
2 tablespoons ginger (crushed)
2 tablespoons celery (finely chopped)
1 tablespoon chili pepper (finely chopped)
400ml/14oz white wine vinegar

(Makes 1L/1¾pt/1qt)

Preparation
30 min

1. Combine all the chopped herbs and vegetables in a deep bowl and mix thoruoughly until well blended. We recommend that you use an electric blender or food processor to ensure that all the herbs and vegetables are finely chopped to the consistency of pesto.

2. Add the white wine vinegar to the mixture and stir thoroughly. The vinegar will preserve the herbs as well as smoothen the paste.

3. Store refrigerated in a sealed container. The paste will last for up to 12 months as the vinegar preserves the ingredients.

Note:
You can be creative with the seasoning by adding other herbs that you like and/or make bigger batches keeping a limited stock in the refrigerator while freezing the rest.

Tip:
The paste is used mainly to marinate any type of meat. The marination can be for as little as 20 minutes to overnight. The paste is also ideal for sauces, stews, omelettes and soups.

HOT PEPPER SAUCE

Most families in Trinidad and Tobago make hot pepper sauce from recipes handed down for generations. A teaspoon or two is added to almost any meal.

400g/14oz hot peppers (washed, chopped with tops removed)
2 large carrots (washed, peeled and chopped)
1 large red onion (chopped)
6 tablespoons white wine vinegar
5 tablespoons American yellow mustard

Note: use an assortment of chilli peppers, combining Scotch bonnet, habanero, cayenne, jalapeño and Thai peppers.
1. Add all the fresh, chopped peppers, carrots and onion into a blender and grind until the ingredients are of a rough, paste consistency.
2. Add the American yellow mustard and white vinegar and purée into a smooth sauce.
3. Transfer the pepper sauce liquid into a sterilised, hermetically sealed jar or other suitable container. Store refrigerated for up to 12 months.

RED PEPPER PASTE

Red pepper paste is the secret ingredient added to several of our Armenian and Middle Eastern recipes. It is also excellent as a dip for traditional dishes such as Vospov Kufteh (see page 139) or spread on warm or toasted bread.

2 large red bell peppers
(seeded and chopped)
1 teaspoon salt
1 tablespoon olive oil

(Makes 170g/6oz)

Preparation	Cooking	Total
15 min	45 min	1 hr

1. Add the red bell peppers into a blender and grind until the peppers are of a rough, paste consistency. Mix in the salt.

2. Transfer into a saucepan and heat over high heat, stirring until the paste starts bubbling.

3. Reduce the heat to simmer for 30-45 minutes, stirring frequently, until the mixture is reduced to the consistency of a purée.

4. Remove from the heat and allow to cool.

5. Transfer the red pepper paste into a sterilised, hermetically sealed jar or a suitable, airtight container. Cover the paste with 1 tablespoon of olive oil, which will act as a natural sealant. Seal the jar and refrigerate.

6. Alternatively, pour the paste into plastic, ice cube trays and freeze. Once frozen, transfer the cubes into sealed, freezer bags for future use. The cubes will last up to 10 months in the freezer.

Tip: add the frozen cubes straight into simmering stews when needed.

HOT PEPPER CHUTNEY

Not to be confused with our Hot Pepper Sauce (see page 13), our unique Hot Pepper Chutney is a hot and sweet condiment, with a subtly fruity hint of apricots.

250g/9oz hot peppers (washed, chopped with tops removed)
250g/9oz carrots (washed, peeled and chopped)
1 large red bell pepper (seeded and chopped)
16 spring onions
8 cloves garlic
1 tablespoon olive oil
1 tablespoon chopped parsley
Juice of 1 lemon
Juice of 1 lime
1 teaspoon ginger (grated)
10 tablespoons caster sugar
3 tablespoons white wine vinegar
1 teaspoon salt
300ml/10½oz water (divided)
250g/9oz soft dried apricots (diced)
40ml/1½oz white rum

(Makes 1¼L/2¼pt/1¼qt)

Preparation	Cooking	Total
15 min	**45 min**	**1 hr**

Note: Use an assortment of chilli peppers, combining Scotch bonnet, habanero, cayenne, jalapeño and Thai peppers. Remove the red bell pepper seeds but keep the hot chilli pepper seeds.

1. Add all of the fresh, chopped peppers, carrots, spring onions and garlic into a blender and grind until the ingredients are of a rough paste consistency.
2. Heat the olive oil in a deep pan over moderate heat. Add the blended ingredients and mix well with a spoon.
3. Mix in the chopped parsley, grated ginger, sugar, white wine vinegar, lemon juice, lime juice, salt and 150ml of water.
4. Bring the mixture to the boil. Reduce the heat and simmer for 45 minutes until the mixture is cooked and of the consistency of chutney.
5. Meanwhile, place the apricots and the remaining 150ml/5¼oz of water into a deep pot. Heat over high heat for 10 minutes or until all the water is absorbed and the apricots are tender but not soggy or mushy.
6. Blend the apricots for only a second using an electric blender. Do not purée. Mix in the rum with a spoon.
7. Stir the apricot and rum mixture into the chutney during the final 5 minutes of cooking.
8. Transfer the hot pepper chutney into a sterilised, hermetically sealed jar or another airtight container. Store refrigerated for up to 12 months.

ONION & MUSTARD MAYO

Our onion and mustard mayo is great with meat, poultry or fish. Perfect with ham on toast. Keep refrigerated for up to 1 week, if you can resist eating it.

1 medium onion
200g/7oz mayonnaise
4 tablespoons American mustard
1 tablespoon dark rum
2 teaspoons lemon juice
½ teaspoon Angostura bitters
½ teaspoon black pepper

1. Dice the onion and put it aside. Note: To avoid irritated eyes, use a very sharp knife and cut the onions in cold water. Alternatively, wear swimming goggles and sing a happy tune while dicing.

2. Put everything except the diced onion in a blender. Blend for about 10 seconds.

3. Stir in the onions. Do not blend.

4. Remove your goggles and enjoy.

BURNT SUGAR SYRUP

Burnt Sugar Syrup, is a bittersweet, smokey-flavoured liquid also known as browning. It is an essential ingredient for authentic Black Cake (see page 157), and traditional Caribbean marinades, gravies, and stews. It's simple to make, all you need is brown sugar and water.

50g/1¾oz soft dark brown sugar
50ml/1¾oz boiling water

(Makes approximately 4 tablespoons of syrup)

Note: in the Caribbean, most households make a few litres of syrup, which they store for future use, as and when needed. Increase the ingredients as required.

Preparation	Cooking	Total
5 min	5 min	10 min

1. Heat the sugar in a deep pan over medium heat until it begins to melt and becomes a light chocolate colour.

2. Remove the pan from the heat and mix in the boiling water. The mixture will sizzle as the water produces steam.

3. Keep stirring until the colour of the mixture darkens into a deep chocolate colour.

4. Return the pan to very low heat and stir continuously for 2-3 minutes or until all the sugar crystals melt completely and the mixture thickens into a syrup.

5. Remove from the heat. Use immediately or leave to cool, then transfer into a sterile, airtight container. **Note: The syrup will thicken even more as it cools. It can be stored in a cool, dark place for at least 12 months.**

NOTES

NOTES

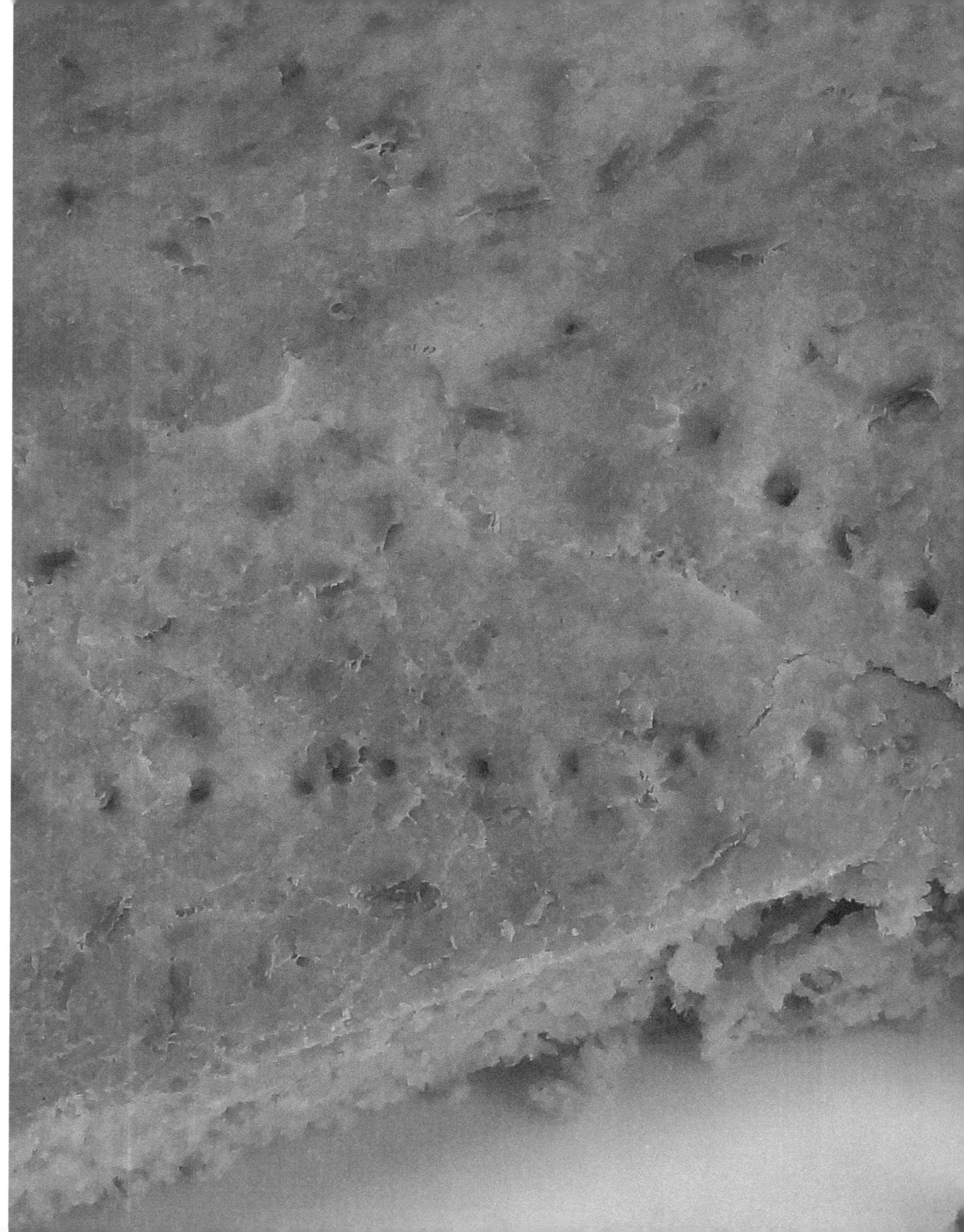

Breads & Breakfast

COCONUT BAKE

Coconut Bake is a hearty, quintessentially Caribbean coconut bread. It is ideal for breakfast or supper and is excellent with a hot beverage. It's great served hot with melted butter or at room temperature with soft cheese. For a special treat, enjoy with a generous slice of our delicious Baked Omelette (see page 35).

400ml/14oz coconut milk
2 tablespoons olive oil
¾ cup grated coconut (optional)
1¼ teaspoon salt
4 cups plain flour
1½ teaspoon bread machine/instant yeast

Serves	Preparation	Cooking	Total
8	1 hr 40 min	20 min	2 hrs

1. Ensure the kneading blade is attached to the bread machine's baking pan.

2. Beginning with the coconut milk, place the carefully measured oil, salt, and grated coconut into the baking pan.

3. Cover the ingredients with flour ensuring that the top of the flour remains dry. Do not stir.

4. The yeast must only be placed on dry flour. So, on top of the flour, make an impression in the centre with a spoon. Then, ensuring that it remains dry, add the yeast into the impression.

5. Select Dough cycle. When the cycle is complete, remove the dough and knead into a round shape. Use a rolling pin to flatten slightly. Create cutting guides by pricking the top with a fork. Bake in a pre-heated oven for 20 minutes at 200°C/390°F.

6. Once baked, carefully remove from the baking pan and cool on a wire rack for 10 minutes.

Note:
For a hands-on approach, add the indredients to a bowl, mix until firm then knead on a floured surface. Leave to rise for an hour, covered with a damp cloth.

COCONUT SWEET BREAD

Coconut Sweet Bread is a Caribbean favourite, especially during holidays. There are several types that differ according to personal taste. Our original recipe for a bread making machine is not as sweet as most of the traditional hands-on variations. It is ideal as a dessert or lightly toasted and buttered for breakfast.

260ml/9oz water
2 tablespoons olive oil
1½ teaspoons salt
3 tablespoons granulated sugar
1 teaspoon Angostura bitters
½ cup grated coconut
2 tablespoons skimmed milk powder
1 teaspoon allspice
3 cups strong white flour
1½ teaspoons bread machine/instant yeast
½ cup mixed fruit
½ cup glacé cherries (halved)
½ cup candied fruit (optional)

Serves	Preparation	Cooking	Total
8	15 min	2 hrs 55 min	3 hrs 10 min

1. Ensure the kneading blade is attached to the bread machine's baking pan.

2. Beginning with the water, place the carefully measured oil, salt, sugar and bitters into the baking pan.

3. Add the grated coconut, skimmed milk powder and allspice. Do not stir.

4. Cover the ingredients with flour ensuring that the top of the flour remains dry. Do not stir.

5. The yeast must only be placed on dry flour. So, on top of the flour, make an impression in the centre with a spoon. Then, ensuring that it remains dry, add the yeast into the impression.

6. Select Sweet, Basic or White cycle. Choose either medium or light crust, according to your preference.

7. Add the mixed fruit, glacé cherries, and candied fruit during the last kneading cycle.

8. Once baked, carefully remove the sweet bread from the baking pan and cool on a wire rack.

DHALPURI

No collection of Caribbean recipes would be complete without roti. Dhalpuri is a type of Trinidadian roti or flatbread of Indian origin that is stuffed with seasoned dhal or yellow split peas. Traditionally, roti is torn by hand and eaten with scoops of curry sauce and pieces of meat. However, the roti wrap, which was first created in South Trinidad during the mid-1940s, is now widely popular.

Serves	Preparation	Cooking	Total
6	1 hr	1 hr	2 hrs

Filling:
150g/5¼oz yellow split peas (stones removed, washed and drained)
1 clove garlic (crushed)
½ teaspoon saffron
Salt to taste
2 cloves garlic (whole)
2 teaspoons ground cumin
¼ teaspoon ground black pepper.

Dough:
400g/14oz plain flour
3 teaspoons baking powder
Water for kneading

Other Ingredients:
50g/1¾oz unsalted butter (melted)
70g/2½oz olive oil

Note:
Traditionally, an enamel mug is used to press down the roti, especially the edges; and to spread grease on the surface of the roti before it is turned.

1. Boil the split peas, crushed garlic, saffron and salt together until the split peas are cooked but firm. Drain and leave to cool.
2. Transfer the cooked split peas to a food processor or blender. Add the remaining ingredients for the filling and blend until fine.
3. Place the flour and baking powder in a mixing bowl and knead into a soft dough. Transfer to a flat, floured surface, knead and roll into a smooth ball. Coat the surface of the ball of dough with olive oil and leave to rest for 15 minutes.
4. Divide the dough into 6 balls. Press the centre of each ball to open up a cavity. Fill each cavity with 3-4 table-spoons of filling then close the dough around the filling. Leave the 6 filled dough balls to rest for 15 minutes.
5. Combine the melted butter with the remaining olive oil on a plate.
6. Heat a large tawa, tava, griddle or frying pan over moderate heat.
7. On a flat, floured surface, use a rolling pin to roll out each dough ball into a roti, approximately 20cm/8in in diameter.
8. Grease the tawa or griddle with a tablespoon of the combined butter and olive oil, then place a roti on the tawa. Grease the top of the roti while cooking. Turn over and repeat. Follow this procedure for each dough ball.
9. Serve immediately with West Indian Chicken Curry (see page 89) or your favourite curry dish.

EGGS & TOMATOES

Food does not have to be complicated to be delicious. This simple recipe for Armenian-style scrambled eggs with tomatoes is a favourite breakfast dish that is ready in fifteen minutes. Serve with toast, sliced baguette, hot pitta bread or Coconut Bake (see page 27) for an unforgettable early morning treat.

2 tablespoons olive oil
½ small onion (finely chopped)
1 clove garlic (crushed)
6 medium free range eggs
2 large tomotoes (peeled and chopped) or 6 cherry tomotoes cut in two pieces (no need to peel)
1 teaspoon paprika or chilli powder
½ teaspoon salt
½ teaspoon ground black pepper

Serves	Preparation	Cooking	Total
4-6	5 min	10 min	15 min

1. Cook the garlic and onions in olive oil, in a large frying pan, over medium heat, for 2 minutes or until they have slighlty softened.

2. Mix in the tomatoes. Cover and cook over low heat until the tomatoes are completely soft and tender.

3. In a separate bowl, beat the eggs together with the salt, black pepper, and paprika or chilli powder.

4. Pour the seasoned eggs into the pan, stir gently, and cook until firm. Voila!

BAKED OMELETTE

For breakfast or brunch, you can't go wrong with our deliciously indulgent Baked Omelette; just add your favourite breakfast bread, and a glass of mango or passion fruit juice for a mouth-watering meal made in paradise.

8 large eggs
4 tablespoons dark rum
2 tablespoons double cream
2 tablespoons green seasoning (see page 11)
1 tablespoon ketchup
1 vegetable stock cube (crushed)
2 teaspoons lemon juice
1 teaspoon celery salt
½ teaspoon hot pepper sauce (see page 13)
1 clove garlic (crushed)
1 dash Angostura bitters
160g/5½oz honey roast ham slices (diced)
80g/3oz grated cheddar cheese
2 tomatoes (diced)
20g/1oz red bell pepper (diced)
20g/1oz green bell pepper (diced)
1 spring onion (after washing, trim roots and ragged top ends then chop into 5mm/¼in pieces)
1 tablespoon olive oil

Serves	Preparation	Cooking	Total
4	15 min	25 min	40 min

1. Put aside the ham, cheese, and vegetables.

2. In a large bowl, whisk the eggs together with the remaining ingredients.

3. Add the ham, cheese, and vegetables. Use a spoon to mix well.

4. Preheat the oven to 200°C/390°F. Pour the olive oil into a baking dish and coat with a brush.

5. Pour the mixture into the prepared baking dish and bake in the oven for 25 minutes, or until the omelette is cooked and has a golden-brown top.

6. Remove the omelette from the oven and serve with warm toast, pitta bread, or Coconut Bake (see page 27).

NOTES

NOTES

Soups

HEARTY SOUP

This soup recipe is for our hearty, family variation of Chinese chicken noodle soup and chicken and sweetcorn soup. Although it can be a starter, we always have it as a main meal. Great for those rainy, cold or wintery days.

2½L/4½pt/2½qt water
1 tablespoon green seasoning (see page 11)
1 teaspoon garlic (crushed)
250g/9oz red lentils (soaked for 1 hour and drained)
700g/1½lb chicken (skinned, boneless, and cubed)
250g/9oz small tomatoes (diced)
100g/3½oz celery (diced)
30g/1oz spring onions (diced)
2 tablespoons tomato ketchup
300g/10½oz new or baby potatoes (peeled)
200g/7oz baby carrots (peeled)
1 teaspoon celery salt
300g/10½oz sweet corn and peppers (drained)
100g/3½oz/2 packets chicken noodle soup mix
150g/5¼oz macaroni
50g/1¾oz spaghetti (broken into short pieces)
1 dash Angostura bitters

Serves	Preparation	Cooking	Total
6-8	30 min	1 hr 30 min	2 hrs

1. Put the chicken, green seasoning, garlic and red lentils into a deep pan of at least 5L capacity. Cover with 2½L of water, stir and bring to the boil over hot heat. Use a mesh strainer or sieve to remove any froth.

2. Reduce the heat to moderate and add the tomatoes, celery, spring onions and ketchup. Cover with a suitable lid and cook for 30 minutes.

3. Add the potatoes and carrots. Cover the pan and cook for 30 minutes.

Note: if using tinned potatoes and carrots, add them at step 4.

4. Gently stir in the celery salt, sweetcorn and peppers and the chicken noodle soup mix. Reduce the heat, cover and simmer for 20 minutes.

5. Stir in the macaroni, spaghetti and Angostura bitters. Cover and simmer for 10 minutes or until the macaroni is cooked.

6. Remove the pan from the heat and leave to stand for 10 minutes. Gently stir and serve.

Tip: The potatoes and pasta will quickly absorb the liquid. Add water, as required, before re-heating.

LENTIL SOUP

Lentil soup is an ancient dish with historical links to Africa, the Middle East, Armenia, Greece, Turkey and India. Delicious and nutritious, it is a good source of protein, fibre, iron and potassium. For a vegetarian alternative, simply omit the pancetta or bacon and use a vegetable stock cube instead of pork.

1 tablespoon olive oil
160g diced smoked pancetta or smoked bacon (divided)
1 medium red onion (finely chopped)
100g red lentils
1¼L water
1 pork stock cube or vegetable stock cube (crushed)
2 large potatoes (washed, peeled and chopped)
2 large carrots (chopped)
Pepper to taste
2 tablespoons dried or fresh coriander (finely chopped)

Serves	Preparation	Cooking	Total
2	10 min	30 min	40 min

1. Place the red lentils into a colander and wash with cool, running water. Transfer to a bowl and soak in cool water for 15 minutes.

2. Meanwhile, heat the olive oil in a deep saucepan over hot heat then add the pancetta and chopped onion. Sauté for a few minutes until the pancetta is crisp and the onion is translucent. Scoop out half of the pancetta from the pot and set aside in a small bowl.

3. Pour in the water and add the stock cube. Drain the lentils and mix into the pot. Bring to the boil for 10 minutes over high heat then add the potatoes and carrots.

4. Reduce the heat and simmer for another 20 minutes or until the vegetables are cooked.

5. Remove from the heat and swizzle or blend with a hand mixer until the soup is smooth.

6. Mix in the coriander and the remaining pancetta. Serve immediately.

CALLALOO

Callaloo is a popular Caribbean dish served in several variations across the Caribbean. The callaloo made in Trinidad and Tobago is a distinctive side dish made with taro leaves, also known as dasheen bush, okra and coconut milk for a truly unique flavour and consistency. Jamaican callaloo, which is similar and more widely available here in the UK, can also be used instead of dasheen.

Serves	Preparation	Cooking	Total
4-6	10 min	30 min	40 min

1 tablespoon olive oil
160g/5½oz smoked pancetta (omit for vegetarian or vegan option)
80g/3oz green bell pepper (finely diced)
60g/2oz white onion (finely diced)
1 clove garlic (crushed)
350g/12¼oz tinned callaloo or dasheen bush/taro leaves
150g/5¼oz okra (fresh or frozen, chopped into 10mm slices, washed and trimmed of stems and ends)
2 tablespoons chives (chopped)
1 tablespoon fresh thyme (chopped)
60ml/2oz water
1 pork stock cube (use vegetable stock cube for vegetarian or vegan option)
Or: fish stock cube with 100g/3½oz crab meat (optional)
1 teaspoon hot pepper sauce (see page 13)
200ml/7oz coconut milk

1. Heat the olive oil in a deep saucepan over hot heat then add the pancetta, bell pepper, onion and garlic. Sauté for a few minutes until the pancetta is crisp and the onion is translucent. Scoop out half of the pancetta from the saucepan and set aside in a small bowl.

2. Add the tinned callaloo, okra, chives and thyme. Cook for a few minutes before adding the water, then cook for 5 minutes.

3. Add the stock cube and crab if desired. Bring to the boil for 10 minutes over high heat then add the hot pepper sauce and coconut milk.

4. Reduce the heat and simmer for another 10 minutes or until the vegetables are cooked.

5. Remove from the heat and swizzle or blend with a hand mixer until a stewlike consistency is achieved.

6. With a spoon, mix in the remaining pancetta and serve immediately.

Note: Cooked ham or smoked bacon can be used instead of the smoked pancetta. However, omit any meat and meat stock for a vegetarian alternative.

NOTES

NOTES

Meat & Poultry

LAHMAJOON

Lahmajoon or Armenian Pizza is a popular dish in Armenia, Turkey, Lebanon, Syria, and in Armenian and Turkish communities throughout the world. It has also gained popularity in Jerusalem due to the migration of Jews from Turkey. This delicious recipe can be made with minced beef or lamb, or without meat as a spicy vegetarian option. Great as a snack, main, or side dish.

Serves	Preparation	Cooking	Total
4-8	15 min	10 min	25 min

Meat Paste:
500g/17½oz lean ground lamb or beef
1 green pepper (finely chopped)
1 large tomato (peeled, seeded, and finely chopped)
1 medium white onion (finely chopped)
50g/1¾oz parsley (chopped)
25g/1oz mint (chopped)
2 cloves garlic (crushed)
2 tablespoons lemon juice
2 tablespoons tomato paste
2 teaspoons paprika
2 teaspoons salt
2 teaspoons pepper
1 teaspoon allspice
1 teaspoon cinnamon

Other Ingredients:
6 flour tortilla wraps (40g/1½oz each)
1 lemon (for garnish)

1. Preheat the oven to 200°C/390°F.

2. Combine the meat, vegetables, herbs and spices in a bowl and knead well until blended into a paste. Your finished paste of 600g/21oz makes 8 Armenian pizzas.

3. Dust baking trays with flour and place 2 or 3 tortillas on each tray, depending on the size of your oven.

4. Evenly spread 75g/2¾oz of meat paste on each tortilla, leaving a 0.6cm/¼in rim or border (see pages 53 and 54).

5. Place your baking trays in the oven and bake for 10 minutes or until the meat is cooked and the tortilla edges begin to lightly brown.

6. Keep the cooked Armenian pizzas stacked on top of each other and cover with a damp cloth to prevent them from becoming too brittle.

7. Squeeze a bit of lemon juice on top and serve hot or at room temperature. Note: The Armenian pizzas can be stacked on top of each other, served individually, or rolled and eaten as delicious wraps.

BOREG

Boreg is a delightful, traditional Armenian baked filled pastry made with tissue-thin sheets of flaky dough known as phyllo (or filo). In Greek, phyllo means "leaf" and sheets of the dough can be found ready made and frozen. Our boreg recipes are quite simple; and once tried, never forgotten.

12 phyllo sheets 480mm x 255mm (19in x 10in)
85g/3oz butter (melted for glazing)

Beef:
2 tablespoons olive oil
400g/14oz beef (minced)
2 medium tomatoes
1 white onion (finely chopped)
50g/1¾oz parsley (chopped)
3 tablespoons pine nuts
1 teaspoon allspice
1 teaspoon salt
½ teaspoon cayenne pepper
½ teaspoon ground black pepper

Cheese:
65g/2¼oz halloumi cheese (grated)
50g/1¾oz cheddar cheese (grated)
50g/1¾oz parsley (chopped)
1 egg (whisked)

Serves	Preparation	Cooking	Total
4-6	30 min	30 min	1 hr

Beef:

1. Heat the olive oil in a frying pan over high heat. Add the chopped onions and cook them for a few minutes until they become translucent.

2. Add the minced beef and reduce the heat to simmer. Cook the beef until almost brown then stir in the tomatoes. If the beef becomes dry and sticky, add a few tablespoons of water.

3. Add the pine nuts and season with salt, cayenne pepper and allspice. Cook for 5-10 minutes on low heat until all of the ingredients have fused together and there is no liquid in the pan.

4. Remove from the heat and leave to cool.

Cheese:

1. Place the combination of grated cheeses into a deep bowl. Gently mix in the chopped parsley and egg until all the ingredients have combined.

Continued on page 59.

BOREG

Continued from page 57.

Spinach & Cheese:
1 tablespoon olive oil
100g/3½oz baby spinach leaves (chopped)
1 small onion (finely chopped)
65g/2¼oz halloumi cheese (grated)
50g/1¾oz cheddar cheese (grated)
½ teaspoon ground black pepper

Note:
Unbaked boregs can be frozen on a baking tray lined with waxed paper or baking parchment. Once frozen, transfer them to a freezer-proof, airtight container and store in the freezer for up to 3 months. However, do not brush the pastry with butter before freezing. You can place them straight into a pre-heated oven from frozen, adding melted butter on top.

Serves	Preparation	Cooking	Total
4-6	30 min	30 min	1 hr

Spinach and Cheese:
1. Heat the olive oil in a frying pan over high heat. Add the baby spinach leaves and cook them for 3-5 minutes until they have wilted.

2. Remove from the heat and leave to cool a little before mixing in the combination of cheeses. Season with pepper only; do not add salt as the cheeses will provide enough saltiness for the fillings.

Wrapping the fillings in the phyllo pastry:
1. Remove two phyllo sheets at a time from the pack and keep the unused sheets covered with a damp kitchen towel

2. Lay the phyllo sheets on a clean work surface, cutting them in half to 240mm x 127.5mm (9½in x 5in)

3. Brush the first half with melted butter then stack the second half on top of it before also brushing it with melted butter. **Note: add the fillings as illustrated on the following pages.**

Baking the boregs:
1. Preheat the oven to 200°C/390°F.

2. Place the boregs on a baking tray lined with parchment. Brush the tops with melted butter and bake for 15-20 minutes or until golden brown.

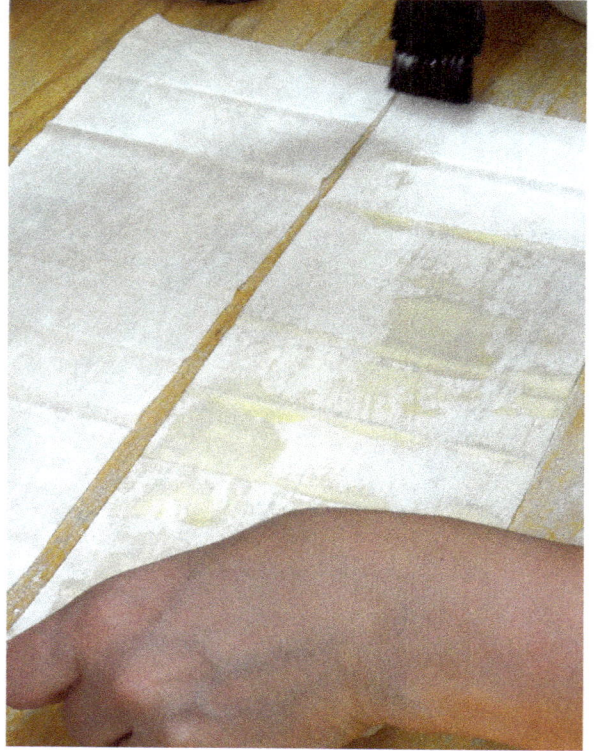

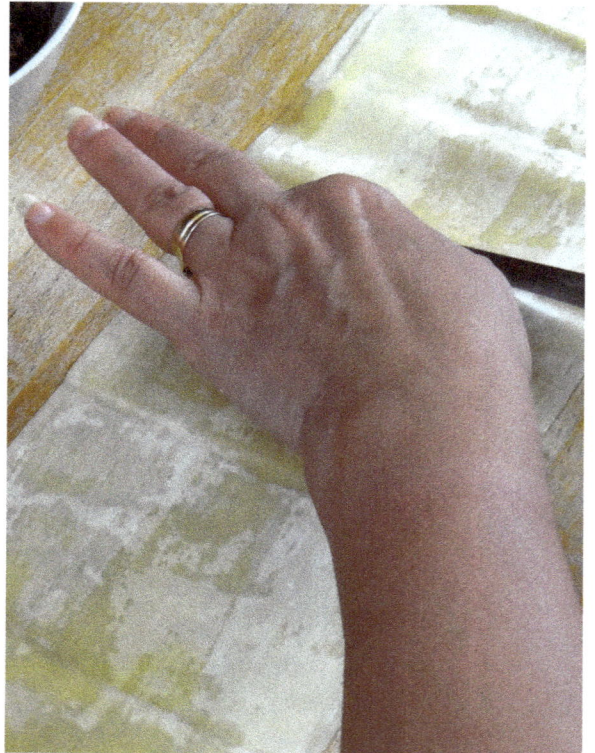

MACARONI PIE

Macaroni Cheese is of English origin and has many variations. In Canada and the United States of America, it's mac and cheese but in Trinidad and Tobago, it's macaroni pie. It can be a main or side dish, with or without beef. This beef version was inspired by my mother's recipe. For a vegetarian variation, simply omit the ground beef and substitute the beef stock with vegetable stock.

500g/17½oz macaroni
2 cloves chopped garlic
½ chopped onion
1 tablespoon green seasoning (see page 11)
1 teaspoon salt
1 teaspoon hot pepper sauce (see page 13)
1 beef stock cube (crushed)
3 tablespoons olive oil (divided)
500g/17½oz ground beef
1 tablespoon burnt sugar syrup (see page 21)
4 eggs
2 tablespoons dark rum
1 teaspoon lemon juice
4 tablespoons tomato ketchup
500g/17½oz grated cheddar cheese (divided)
½ teaspoon black pepper
1 dash Angostura bitters

Serves	Preparation	Cooking	Total
6	15 min	45 min	1 hr

1. Cook the macaroni in a large pan of boiling, salted water but reduce the recommended cooking time by 2 minutes. Once cooked, drain using a colander then transfer to a large mixing bowl.

2. While the macaroni boils, sauté the garlic, onion, green seasoning, salt, hot pepper sauce and beef stock for 2 minutes, with 2 tablespoons of olive oil.

3. Add the ground beef and burnt sugar syrup to the saucepan with the sautéed seasoning and cook thoroughly, stirring occasionally.

4. Prepare a large baking dish by brushing with 1 table-spoon of olive oil and sprinkling in 50g/1¾oz of the grated cheddar cheese. Heat the oven to 200°C/390°F.

5. Whisk the eggs, dark rum, lemon juice and ketchup in a measuring jug and add a dash of Angostura bitters. Pour the whisked egg mixture over the hot macaroni and mix well using a large spoon.

6. Stir 300g/10½oz of grated cheddar with the macaroni and the whisked egg. Add the cooked ground beef, and mix well before spooning into the prepared baking dish.

7. Sprinkle the remaining cheddar cheese on top, dust with black pepper, and bake in the oven for 30 minutes.

BAKED AUBERGINE CASSEROLE

With its origins in Sri Lanka and India, the aubergine or eggplant is a popular ingredient in the cuisines of Armenia, the Middle East, the Meditteranean and the Caribbean. Our Baked Aubergine Casserole is excellent with Bulgur Pilaf (see page 133).

3 tablespoons olive oil (divided)
1 large onion (finely chopped)
2 cloves garlic (crushed)
400g/14oz beef (minced)
400g/14oz tinned tomatoes (chopped)
1 tablespoon red pepper paste (see page 15)
4 tablespoons parsley (chopped)
2 teaspoons mixed spices
1 teaspoon paprika
Salt and ground black pepper to taste
4 aubergines cut into 2cm/¾in slices

Sauce:
150g/5¼oz tinned chopped tomatoes
50ml/1¾oz boiling water
2 teaspoons tomato paste
½ vegetable stock cube

Serves	Preparation	Cooking	Total
4-6	20 min	1 hr	1 hr 20 min

1. Heat 1 tablespoon of olive oil in a deep saucepan over high heat and add the onion and garlic. Sauté for a few minutes until the onion becomes translucent.
2. Add the minced beef. Cook until it begins to brown then add the tomatoes. If the beef becomes dry and sticky, add a few tablespoons of water.
3. Mix in the red pepper paste, chopped parsley, mixed spices and paprika. Season with salt and pepper to taste. Reduce the heat to simmer for 10 minutes.
4. Meanwhile, heat the remaining olive oil in a frying pan over high heat. Arrange a few aubergine slices flat in the pan, ensuring they do not overlap. Lightly fry each side then transfer the slices to a paper towel to soak up any excess oil. Repeat this process until all the aubergine slices are half cooked. **Note: use only a small amount of oil to avoid the dish becoming too oily.**
5. Preheat the oven to 200°C/390°F.
6. Place half of the cooked minced beef and tomatoes into a casserole dish that is at least 64mm/2½in deep. Evenly cover the beef and tomatoes with half of the aubergine slices. Add the remaining beef and tomatoes and blanket with the remaining aubergine slices. Mix the sauce ingredients together in a mixing jug, then slowly and evenly pour the sauce over the casserole.
7. Cover the casserole with a lid or baking foil and place it into the oven. Bake for 30 minutes, then uncover and bake for a further 20 minutes.

ARMENIAN SHISH KOFTE

Shish (skewer) Kofte (kebab) is a popular Turkish and Armenian dish made with grilled minced meat and finely chopped herbs. It is excellent with Aubergine Salad (see page 119), Almond & Sultana Pilaf (see page 129), Bulgur Pilaf (see page 133) or bread.

50g/1¾oz bulgur or cracked wheat (medium grain)
150g/5¼oz minced beef
½ small onion (finely chopped)
30g/1oz pine nuts (chopped)
1 tablespoon red pepper paste (see page 15)
½ teaspoon cumin
½ teaspoon coriander
½ teaspoon cinnamon
½ teaspoon allspice
1 teaspoon salt
¼ teaspoon black pepper
1 egg (beaten)
1 tablespoon olive oil

Serves	Preparation	Cooking	Total
1-2	10 min	10 min	20 min

1. Soak the bulgur in cold water to soften. After 30 minutes, drain into a mixing bowl, ensuring that no excess water remains.

2. Add the minced beef, and the remaining ingredients, including the beaten egg, then thoroughly mix by hand.

3. Preheat the oven to 200°C/390°F.

4. Roll half of the beef mixture into the shape of a long sausage and skewer. Repeat the process for a second skewer.

5. Place the skewers on an oiled grill and cook in the oven for 10 minutes, turning once after the first 5 minutes.

6. Serve with pitta bread and any of the salads we have included in this recipe book.

DOLMA

Dolma is a much-loved, traditional Armenian stuffed vegetable dish, which is also popular in the Middle East and neighbouring regions. We've chosen a variety of vegetables to give the dish different textures and flavours. If you prefer to use one or two vegetables, adjust your ingredient amounts accordingly. For a vegetarian variation, omit the minced meat or replace with minced sultanas.

Filling (divided):
450g/16oz lean ground lamb or beef
100g/4oz long grain rice (washed and drained)
3 large tomatoes (finely chopped)
I large onion (finely chopped)
1 clove garlic (crushed)
3 tablespoons fresh mint leaves (finely chopped)
3 tablespoons parsley leaves (finely chopped)
2 tablespoons red pepper paste (see page 15)
3 teaspoons salt
2 teaspoons black pepper
1 teaspoon paprika

Sauce (divided):
400g/14oz/1 tin chopped tomatoes
150ml/5¼oz boiling water
Juice of 3 lemons
4 teaspoons tomato paste
1 lamb, beef or vegetable stock cube

Serves	Preparation	Cooking	Total
6-8	40 min	1 hr 20 min	2 hrs

1. Place the minced meat, rice, and tomatoes into a deep bowl and mix thoroughly by hand.
2. Add the remaining ingredients and mix again.
Note: the rice in the filling will expand when cooked, so do not completely fill the vegetables.

To stuff the peppers:
Cut off the top sections of the peppers. Using a fruit scoop, melon baller or suitable corer, scoop out any seeds and excess fresh from inside of the peppers and their top sections. Set aside the top sections, which will be put back on top of the peppers after they have been stuffed. Spoon the filling into the peppers until they are ¾ filled, then replace the tops of the peppers.
To stuff the aubergines:
Cut off and discard the top sections of the aubergines. Using a fruit scoop, melon baller or suitable corer, scoop out the flesh and seeds from each aubergine. Leave approximately 10mm of flesh on the interior walls. Spoon the filling into the aubergines until they are ¾ filled.
To stuff the courgettes:
Follow the procedure for the aubergines.
To stuff the vine and cabbage leaves:
See page 72.

Continued on page 71.

DOLMA

Continued from page 69.

Vegetables:
2 small aubergines
2 small courgettes
3 bell peppers - red,
green, yellow, orange or
black
10 grapevine leaves (fresh
or preserved)
5 cabbage leaves (boiled
for 5 minutes, removed
and left to cool)

Note:
Use a paring knife to
remove the entire core
from the head of the
cabbage. Place the whole
cabbage into a large pot
of boiling water for 5
minutes or until the
outer leaves soften. Once
the outer leaves become
pliable, remove the
cabbage from the boiling
water, leave it to cool for
a few minutes before
carefully peeling off the
outer leaves. If required,
repeat this process until
you have removed 5
leaves.

Serves	Preparation	Cooking	Total
6-8	40 min	1 hr 20 min	2 hrs

To cook the stuffed aubergines and courgettes:
Carefully place the stuffed aubergines and courgettes side by side into a deep pan. Pour approximately 200ml/7oz of the tomato and stock sauce over the aubergines. Cover the pan and cook over moderate heat for an hour, or until the vegetables are cooked and juices flow when the vegetables are pierced with the tip of a sharp knife. Add water if required.

To cook the stuffed peppers:
Preheat the oven to 200°C/390°F. Place the stuffed peppers upright into a deep oven casserole dish that has been brushed with olive oil. Pour approximately 200ml/7oz of the tomato and stock sauce over the peppers. Cover the dish with a lid or baking foil and cook in the oven for an hour. Remove the lid and cook for another 15-20 minutes, or until the peppers are cooked and lightly crisped.

To cook the stuffed vine and cabbage leaves:
Heat 2 tablespoons of olive oil in a deep saucepan over moderate heat. Fill the base of the pan with the stuffed vine and cabbage leaves placed seam down, then stack the rest on top of each other. Pour enough of the tomato and stock sauce to cover all but the top layer of stuffed leaves. Cover the pan, reduce heat to simmer for an hour. Check regularly, adding water if required.

Serve with Jajukh (see page 125).

71

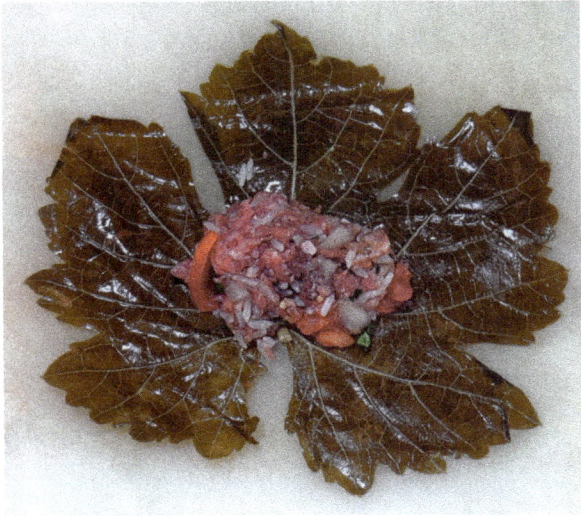

MEATBALLS IN RUM SAUCE

Meatballs in Rum Sauce is our own variation of the Italian classic ragù alla bolognese. It's unlikely you've tasted anything quite like our distinctive recipe. Have it with penne or fusilli, it's absolutely gorgeous.

1kg/2¼lb/36 beef meat-balls

Serves	Preparation	Cooking	Total
6	5 min	20 min	25 min

Seasoning:
2 tablespoons olive oil
1 tablespoon green seasoning (see page 11)
1 tablespoon burnt sugar syrup (see page 21)
2 tablespoons Italian seasoning (or
1 tablespoon oregano
2 teaspoons thyme
1 teaspoon parsley
1 teaspoon rosemary)
1 teaspoon hot pepper sauce (see page 13)
2 cloves garlic (chopped)
1 beef stock cube (crushed)

Sauce:
1 tin/400g/14oz chopped tomatoes
4 tablespoons tomato ketchup
4 tablespoons dark rum
1 dash Angostura bitters

Garnish:
6 sprigs parsley

1. Heat the olive oil in a deep pan over moderate heat. Add the seasoning then add the meatballs.

2. Stirring gently and frequently, try not to crush or break the meatballs. Cook for 15 minutes or until the meat has darkened and its juices run clear.

3. Pour the sauce over the meatballs, stirring gently. Cover the pan and reduce the heat to simmer for 5 minutes.

4. With a large spoon, scoop out 6 meatballs per person, place on plates and cover with generous lashings of sauce. Garnish with parsley.

5. Serve with penne, fusilli, linguine or spaghetti.

KUBBA HAMUTH

Known by several regional pronunciations, kubba is a traditional Levantine dish, often considered the national dish of several Middle Eastern countries. Kubba Hamuth, or sour dumplings, is an ancient Chaldean recipe that is particularly popular in Iraq. Similar to dumplings boiled in a rich broth, it is a hearty, warming dish. Be sure to add lemon juice. If it isn't sour, it isn't Kubba Hamuth.

Serves	Preparation	Cooking	Total
4-6	30 min	1 hr	1 hr 30 min

Outer Shell:
200g/7oz rice flour
200g/7oz lamb or beef (minced)
1 small onion (chopped)
140ml/5oz cold water
1 teaspoon salt
Black pepper to taste

Filling:
70g/2½oz lamb or beef (minced)
1 teaspoon salt
½ teaspoon ground cumin
½ teaspoon ground coriander
½ teaspoon allspice
Black pepper to taste

Broth:
1 tablespoon olive oil
1 small onion (chopped)
1 clove garlic (crushed)
500g/17½oz passata
400ml/14oz water
1 vegetable stock cube

Garnish:
1½ tablespoons dried mint
1½ tablespoons lemon juice

Outer Shell:
Use a food processor to mix the outer shell ingredients together into a sticky paste. Transfer the paste to a bowl and set aside.

Filling:
Use a food processor to mix the filling ingredients together. Transfer the mixture to a bowl and set aside.

Kubba:
1. Wet your palms with cold water. Take around 50g/1¾oz of the outer shell paste and make a small ball. Using your thumb, hollow out the centre of the ball, add a heaped teaspoon of the filling, then close up the ball ensuring all the filling is contained. Wet your hands if the ball becomes sticky. Roll the ball into a torpedo-shaped kubba. Repeat this process to make 12 kubbas or until the mixtures are used up.

2. Arrange the kubbas on a tray so that they do not touch each other. Place the tray in the freezer for around 45 minutes or until the kubbas harden in shape.

Broth:
1. Heat the olive oil in a deep pan over moderate heat, then add the onion and garlic. Stir fry until the onion is soft but not brown. Mix in the passata, water, and stock, then reduce the heat to simmer for 30 minutes.

2. Transfer the kubbas, one at a time, from the freezer to the cooking broth. Mix them gently, ensuring that they do not stick together or to the bottom of the pan. Cover and simmer for 30 minutes. Garnish and serve.

LAMB & WHITE BEAN STEW

Our variation of a popular Armenian stew calls for butter beans instead of the traditional green beans. You can replace the lamb with diced beef or pork. Or substitute the butter beans with green beans, okra, courgettes, aubergines or your favourite vegetable. Inspired by a recipe from The Cuisine of Armenia by Sonia Uvezian.

3 tablespoons olive oil
I large white onion (finely chopped)
2 cloves garlic (crushed)
750g/1¾lb diced lamb leg steak
450g/16oz/1 tin chopped tomatoes
1 tablespoon tomato paste
1 tablespoon red pepper paste (see page 15)
50ml/1¾oz lamb stock
1 teaspoon cumin
1 teaspoon coriander
1 teaspoon salt
1 teaspoon black pepper
1 teaspoon paprika
1 teaspoon ground allspice
400g/14oz/1 tin your choice of white beans [butter beans/cannellini beans/haricot beans] (drained and washed under cool running water)

Serves	Preparation	Cooking	Total
4-6	10 min	1 hr 20 min	1 hr 30 min

1. Heat the olive oil in a large pan over moderate heat. Add the chopped onion and 1 of the cloves of garlic. Stir fry until the onion is soft but not brown.

2. Stir in the diced lamb and sauté until darkened throughout.

3. Add the chopped tomatoes, tomato paste, red pepper paste, lamb stock and the remaining crushed garlic. Stir well, then add all the spices. Salt to taste and stir again.

4. Bring to the boil, put the lid on the pan and reduce the heat to low. Simmer for 1 hour or until the lamb is tender.

Note: You may need to add more stock in order to maintain the sauce and keep the lamb moist and juicy. During the first 30 minutes of cooking, add more salt and pepper if required.

5. Stir in your choice of white beans and cook for a further 20 minutes or until the beans are soft but not overcooked or mushy.

6. Serve with Almond & Sultana Pilaf (see page 129) or Bulgur Pilaf (see page 133).

LAMB & APRICOT KEBAB

Our recipe combines the Bedouin/Arabic tradition of cooking meat with fruit, using ingredients popular among Armenians. Lamb, their most popular meat, is a basic feature of Armenian cuisine. The apricot or Armenian plum is a symbol of Armenian nationality dating back thousands of years; and spices such as cumin, coriander, and bay leaves are integral to many beloved Armenian dishes.

Lamb Marinade:
2 tablespoons brandy
1 tablespoon olive oil
1 clove garlic (crushed)
1 teaspoon lemon juice
½ teaspoon paprika
½ teaspoon ground cumin
½ teaspoon ground coriander
½ teaspoon onion powder
1 teaspoon salt
1 pinch black pepper

Apricot Marinade:
2 tablespoons brandy

Kebabs:
250g/9oz lamb leg steak (diced)
10 whole dried apricots
10 bay leaves (fresh or dried)

Serves	Preparation	Cooking	Total
2	10 min	10 min	20 min

1. Place the diced lamb into a large bowl, add the lamb marinade and mix together with your hands until all the lamb chunks are evenly coated. Cover the bowl with a lid or cling film. Marinate in the refrigerator for a minimum of 2 hours, or ideally overnight.

2. Place the dried apricots into a small bowl and pour the brandy over them. Mix thoroughly with a spoon to ensure that the brandy soaks all the apricots. Cover the bowl with a lid or cling film. Marinate at room temperature for a minimum of 2 hours, or ideally overnight.

3. If using wooden or bamboo skewers, soak 2 of them in water for a minimum of 30 minutes or overnight.

4. Preheat the oven to 200°C/390°F. Brush a grilling rack and 2 skewers with olive oil (if using metal skewers). Thread a lamb chunk, followed by an apricot, and then a bay leaf. Continue this process to fill 2 skewers each with 5 lamb chunks, 5 apricots and 5 bay leaves.

5. Place the kebabs on the grilling rack and grill for 10 minutes, turning once, until the lamb is evenly cooked.

6. Serve with warm pitta bread, Hot Pepper Chutney (see page 17), and Jajukh (see page 125).

PORK & PRUNE KEBAB

Drenched with rum and a dash of Angostura bitters, our Pork & Prune Kebab recipe has a distinctly Caribbean flavour.

Pork Marinade:
2 tablespoons rum
1 tablespoon olive oil
1 dash Angostura bitters
1 clove garlic (crushed)
½ teaspoon hot pepper
sauce (see page 13)
½ teaspoon allspice
½ teaspoon grated ginger
1 teaspoon salt
1 pinch black pepper

Prune Marinade:
2 tablespoons rum

Kebabs:
250g/9oz pork (diced)
10 prunes (pitted)
10 lime slices (halved)

Serves	Preparation	Cooking	Total
2	10 min	10 min	20 min

1. Place the diced pork into a large bowl, add the pork marinade and mix together with your hands until all the pork chunks are evenly coated. Cover the bowl with a lid or cling film. Marinate in the refrigerator for a minimum of 2 hours, or ideally overnight.

2. Place the dried prunes into a small bowl and pour the rum over them. Mix thoroughly with a spoon to ensure that the rum soaks all the prunes. Cover the bowl with a lid or cling film. Marinate at room temperature for a minimum of 2 hours, or ideally overnight.

3. If using wooden or bamboo skewers, soak 2 of them in water for a minimum of 30 minutes or overnight.

4. Preheat the oven to 200°C/390°F. Brush a grilling rack and 2 skewers with olive oil (if using metal skewers). Thread a pork chunk, followed by a prune, and then a lime slice. Continue this process to fill 2 skewers each with 5 pork chunks, 5 prunes, and 5 lime slices.

5. Place the kebabs on the grilling rack and grill for 10 minutes, turning once, until the pork is evenly cooked.

6. Serve with Okra Stew (see page 135) and Rice & Peas (see page 131) or Bulgur Pilaf (see page 133).

GRILLED PORK & LIME

Our Grilled Pork and Lime recipe has just enough tangy lime to offset the pork's natural sweetness. Nice with Tabouleh (see page 117) or Rice & Peas (see page 131). Great with Callaloo (see page 45) or Mixed Bean Salad (see page 127).

Marinade:
4 limes (halved, juiced then quartered)- set aside the spent lime shells for garnishing the pork
2 tablespoons dark honey
2 tablespoons dark rum
1 tablespoon extra virgin olive oil
1 tablespoon green seasoning (see page 11)
2 teaspoons ginger (crushed)
1 teaspoon garlic (chopped)
1 teaspoon celery salt
1 teaspoon Angostura bitters
½ teaspoon hot chilli pepper

Other Ingredients:
600g/1¼lb/6 pork loin chops
1 pork stock cube (crushed)

Garnish:
2 limes (sliced)

Serves	Preparation	Cooking	Total
4-6	15 min	30 min	45 min

1. Place the pork chops into a large bowl and rub the crushed stock cube into them. Add the marinade and mix with your hands until all the pork is evenly coated. Cover the bowl with a lid or cling film. Marinate in the refrigerator for a minimum of 2 hours, or ideally overnight.

2. Preheat the oven to 200°C/390°F.

3. Line the bottom of an oven grill pan with baking foil then cover with the grill.

4. Arrange the marinated pork chops horizontally on the grill. Top with the spent lime shells placed so that they can act as a receptacle for liquid and moisture. Use a tablespoon to bathe the tops of the pork chops with ¾ ¾ of the remaining marinade. See page 85.

5. Grill in the oven for 10 minutes. Bathe with the remaining marinade and cook for another 20 minutes or until golden brown.

6. Immediately remove the pork chops from the oven to prevent them from becoming too dry.

7. Season to taste. Serve garnished with parsley, slices of lime and the grilled lime shells.

CARIBBEAN CHICKEN STEW

Delightfully spicy Chicken Stew is a staple in the Caribbean where it has many variations. The secret of our Trinidad style recipe is in the sauce and for the fullest flavour we highly recommend that you marinade the chicken overnight. Highly versatile, it can be served with a myriad of side dishes including Rice & Peas (see page 131), Macaroni Pie (see page 63), and Tabouleh (see page 117).

Marinade:
8 large tomatoes (finely chopped)
5 tablespoons green seasoning (see page 11)
5 tablespoons thyme and/or oregano (optional)
4 tablespoons dark rum
3 tablespoons fresh ginger (grated)
2 tablespoons sea salt
1 tablespoon black pepper
2 red bell peppers (finely chopped)
2 large onions (finely chopped)
4 cloves garlic (crushed)
2 teaspoons hot pepper sauce (see page 13)
1 teaspoon celery salt

Other Ingredients:
2kg/4½lb skinned chicken thighs on the bone
3 tablespoons olive oil
2 tablespoons burnt sugar syrup (see page 21)

Serves	Preparation	Cooking	Total
6	15 min	1 hr 15 min	1 hr 30 min

1. Place the chicken into a large bowl, add the marinade and mix with your hands until all the chicken pieces are evenly coated. Cover the bowl with a lid or cling film. Marinate in the refrigerator for a minimum of 2 hours, or ideally overnight.

2. Heat the olive oil and burnt sugar syrup in a large pan over hot heat and stir.

3. Reduce the heat. Add only the chicken (without excess marinade) and cook until any liquid dries out.

4. Scoop out only the remaining vegetables and herbs from the marinade, add to the pan and mix. Add only enough liquid from the marinade to keep the chicken moist.

5. Bring to the boil for 2 minutes then cover the pan with its lid. Reduce the heat and slowly simmer for 1 hour or until the chicken is tender. **Note: You may need to add more liquid from the marinade to keep the sauce moist and the chicken juicy. Mix the chicken carefully to avoid shredding. Halfway through cooking, add salt to taste.**

Optional:
If you like a bit of fire in your chicken, add more hot pepper sauce.

WEST INDIAN CHICKEN CURRY

For our authentic West Indian Chicken Curry, we use curry powder that is made in Trinidad and Tobago. It has a distinctive flavour and aroma. However, if you cannot find West Indian curry powder, have no fear, your curry will still be delicious if any high quality, locally available brand is used. Serve with basmati rice or Dhalpuri (see page 31).

Marinade:
1 large white onion (finely chopped)
3 large tomatoes (finely chopped)
2 cloves garlic (crushed)
2 tablespoons fresh ginger (grated)
4 tablespoons green seasoning (see page 11)
1 teaspoon hot pepper sauce (see page 13)
4 tablespoons salt
2 tablespoons black pepper

Other Ingredients:
3 tablespoons olive oil
4 tablespoons curry powder
3 teaspoons ground turmeric
1kg/2lb skinned chicken thighs on the bone
500g/17½oz potatoes (peeled, chopped into 13mm/½in squares, and washed under cold running water)

Garnish:
Fresh coriander leaves

Serves	Preparation	Cooking	Total
4	15 min	1 hr 30 min	1 hr 45 min

1. Place the chicken into a large bowl, add the marinade and mix with your hands until all the chicken pieces are evenly coated. Cover the bowl with a lid or cling film. Marinate in the refrigerator for a minimum of 2 hours, or ideally overnight.

2. Heat the olive oil in a large pan over fairly hot heat. Add the curry powder and turmeric, then mix thoroughly with a spoon.

3. Add only the chicken (without excess marinade) and stir until evenly coated with curry. Reduce the heat and cook until any liquid dries out.

4. Stir in the remaining marinade and 200ml/7oz of hot water. Note: To avoid the sauce being too watery, do not add hot water if there is excessive liquid in the marinade. Try to keep the combined marinade and water to around 300ml/10½oz.

5. Bring to the boil, cover, reduce heat and simmer for 30 minutes. Add the potatoes and simmer another 30 minutes until the chicken is tender.
Note: You may need to add water to replenish the sauce and keep the chicken moist and juicy. Mix the chicken thighs carefully to avoid shredding. Taste the chicken during the first 30 minutes of simmering and add salt and pepper to taste.

GRILLED MANGO CHICKEN

Our original Grilled Mango Chicken recipe is juicy, spicy and delicious with a hint of fruitiness. It's great for a quick Caribbean fix, or for banishing the blues on an overcast day. Grilled Mango Chicken is particularly excellent with Rice & Peas (see page 131), Tabouleh (see page 117) or Pasta Stock (see page 128) and Jajukh (see page 125).

Marinade:
4 tablespoons mango juice
4 tablespoons mango chutney
2 tablespoons balsamic vinegar glaze
2 tablespoons dark rum
1 tablespoon extra virgin olive oil
1 tablespoon dark honey
1 tablespoon green seasoning (see page 11)
1 clove garlic (chopped)
1 teaspoon celery salt
1 teaspoon red chilli peppers (chopped)
1 teaspoon Angostura bitters
½ teaspoon hot pepper sauce (see page 13)

Other Ingredients:
4 skinless, boneless chicken breasts

Serves	Preparation	Cooking	Total
4	15 min	30 min	45 min

1. Place the chicken breasts into a large bowl, add the marinade and mix with your hands until all the chicken pieces are evenly coated. Cover the bowl with a lid or cling film. Marinate in the refrigerator for a minimum of 2 hours, or ideally overnight.

2. Preheat the oven to 200°C/390°F.

3. Line the bottom of an oven grill pan with baking foil then cover with the grill.

4. Arrange the marinated chicken breasts horizontally on the grill. Using a tablespoon, coat the tops of the chicken with half of any remaining marinade.

5. Grill in the oven for 20 minutes.

6. Turn over the chicken pieces and coat the tops with the rest of the marinade.

7. Raise the temperature to 220°C/430°F and grill for 10 minutes or until cooked.

8. Immediately remove the chicken from the oven to prevent it from becoming too dry.

Note: for a fruitier experience, add more mango chutney to taste.

RUM & RED PEPPERS CHICKEN

Our original recipe for Rum & Red Peppers Chicken uses our red bell pepper infusion (see page 187). The rum ensures that the grilled chicken is very tender and the red peppers are brimming with its distinctive flavour. Rum & Red Peppers Chicken is excellent with Baked Marinated Pulses (see page 128) and Rice & Peas (see page 131) or Almond & Sultana Pilaf (see page 129).

Marinade:
8 tablespoons Rum & Red Peppers (see page 187)
2 tablespoons green seasoning (see page 11)
1 tablespoon olive oil
1 tablespoon red pepper paste (see page 15)
1 tablespoon caster sugar

Other Ingredients:
800g/1¾lb skinless, boneless chicken breasts

Serves	Preparation	Cooking	Total
4-6	15 min	30 min	45 min

1. Place the chicken breasts into a large bowl, add the marinade and mix with your hands until all the chicken pieces are evenly coated. Cover the bowl with a lid or cling film. Marinate in the refrigerator for a minimum of 2 hours, or ideally overnight.

2. Preheat the oven to 200°C/390°F.

3. Line the bottom of an oven grill pan with baking foil then cover with the grill.

4. Arrange the marinated chicken breasts horizontally on the grill, bone side up; and top with red peppers from the Rum & Red Peppers infusion. Using a tablespoon, coat the tops of the chicken with any remaining marinade.

5. Grill in the oven for 30 minutes or until the chicken is cooked and golden brown.

6. Immediately remove the chicken from the oven to prevent it from becoming too dry.

NOTES

NOTES

Fish & Seafood

COD KEBAB & SUMAC SALSA

Sumac is a crimson, powdered spice, with a tangy, lemony flavour. Traditionally used in Middle Eastern cuisine, it is often combined with chopped onions as an accompaniment to grilled meats. Sumac has medicinal properties and is readily available online or in most supermarkets and herb shops. Enjoy our new recipe.

Serves	Preparation	Cooking	Total
2	15 min	15 min	30 min

Marinade:
2 tablespoons fresh coriander (chopped)
1 tablespoon olive oil
Juice of ½ lime
1 clove garlic (crushed)
1 teaspoon ground cumin
1 teaspoon ground coriander
½ teaspoon dried chillis (crushed)
¼ teaspoon paprika powder
Salt to taste

Kebabs:
260g/9¼oz cod fillet (skinless and boneless)
2 lemons (sliced)

Salsa:
¼ bell pepper (cored and diced)
½ medium tomato (diced)
1 red chilli pepper (seeded and finely chopped)
2 tablespoons fresh coriander (finely chopped)
1 teaspoon sumac
1½ tablespoons red onions (finely chopped)
Salt to taste

1. Cut the cod into ½ inch cubes, place the cubes into a bowl, and add the marinade. With your hands, gently mix the marinade into the cod, ensuring that the fragile cod chunks do not break. Once all the chunks are evenly coated, cover the bowl with a lid or cling film. Marinate in the refrigerator for a minimum of 2 hours, or ideally overnight.

2. If using wooden or bamboo skewers, soak 2 of them in water for a minimum of 30 minutes or overnight.

3. Preheat the oven to 200°C/390°F. Brush a grilling rack and 2 skewers with olive oil (if using metal skewers). Gently thread the cod chunks and lemon slices onto the skewers.

4. Gently place the kebabs on the grilling rack and grill for 10-15 minutes, carefully turning once, until the soft, fragile cod is evenly cooked.

5. To make the salsa, place all the salsa ingredients in a small bowl and thoroughly mix them together.

6. Remove the cod kebabs from the oven and lay them on a dish together with a generous helping of salsa.

Note: as an alternative, the cod kebabs can be barbecued instead of grilled.

SALSA SALMON

Our scrumptious new recipe is quick, easy to make, and ideal as a romantic meal for two. Among their many health benefits, mango and pomegranate are known to prevent cancer and lower cholesterol. Sweet, tart, and juicy, pomegranate seeds are also reputed to be an aphrodisiac, while nutrient-dense salmon, bristling with omega-3 fatty acids, is an excellent brain food.

Marinade:
2 teaspoons lime juice
1 teaspoon garlic (crushed)
1 teaspoon grated ginger
1 teaspoon salt
½ teaspoon hot pepper sauce (see page 13)
½ teaspoon allspice

Salsa:
80g/3oz mango (peeled and diced)
80g/3oz pomegranate seeds
40g/1½oz orange bell pepper (diced)
1 tablespoon lime juice
½ teaspoon salt

Other Ingredients:
300g/10½oz salmon (two boneless fillets)
2 tablespoons olive oil

Serves	Preparation	Cooking	Total
2	10 min	6 min	16 min

1. Wash the salmon fillets with cold running water, place them into a bowl, add the marinade and mix with your hands until the salmon fillets are evenly coated. Cover the bowl with a lid or cling film, and marinate in the refrigerator for a minimum of 2 hours, or ideally overnight.

2. Combine the salsa ingredients together in a small serving bowl and set aside.

3. Preheat the grill to 200°C/390°F.

4. Heat the olive oil in an ovenproof saucepan over fairly hot heat. Add the salmon fillets, and cook each side of them for about 30 seconds or so.

5. Turn the salmon fillets skin-side up and place the saucepan under the grill. Grill the salmon for 3 minutes, carefully turn them skin-side down and grill for 2 minutes. Do not overcook - salmon can quickly dry out under a hot grill.

6. Immediately serve the salmon fillets with the salsa.

CARIBBEAN SEA BREAM

The name 'bream' applies to a confusing array of narrow, deep-bodied fish. However, all are highly favoured for their coarse and succulent flesh, and delicious, lingering after-taste. Sea bream is also an excellent substitute for red snapper or sea bass. Delicious with rice or green salad.

340g/12oz whole sea bream, (cleaned and gutted)
5 tablespoons green seasoning (see page 11)

Sauce:
2 tablespoons olive oil
2 teaspoons lime juice
2 teaspoons honey
½ red bell pepper (cored and finely chopped)
½ onion (finely chopped)
1 red chilli (finely chopped)
2 teaspoons fresh ginger (grated)
1 teaspoon allspice
1 teaspoon salt

Garnish:
2 onion slices
1 red bell pepper (cored and sliced into rings)

Serves	Preparation	Cooking	Total
4	15 min	1 hr	1 hr 15 min

1. Wash the sea bream and score it diagonally, 4 times on each side.

2. Transfer the sea bream to a suitable container, and generously season it with the green seasoning. Ensure that the scores, surface, and body cavity are all thoroughly coated. Cover the bowl with a lid or cling film, and marinate in the refrigerator for a minimum of 2 hours, or ideally overnight.

3. Grease a rectangular, ovenproof casserole dish with 1 tablespoon of olive oil. Place 2 onion rings on either side of the casserole dish then add 4 red bell pepper rings to the dish.

4. Place the sea bream so that its head and tail are resting on the onion slices, and its body is supported by the red bell pepper rings.

5. Preheat the oven to 200°C/390°F.

6. Place all the sauce ingredients into a blender or food processor and blend thoroughly. Add more olive oil if required.

7. Pour the sauce over the sea bream and cover the casserole dish with a lid or baking foil. Place the dish in the oven and bake for 45 minutes. Remove the lid or foil, and bake for another 15 minutes, to add crispness to the skin of the sea bream.

FISH CURRY

With one of the most cosmopolitan populations on Earth, it comes as no surprise that the cuisine of Trinidad and Tobago is among the most diverse in the world. Enjoy these simple, mouth-watering, Indo-Trinidadian fish curry variations. Delicious garnished with fresh, chopped coriander leaves and served with basmati rice or Rice & Peas (see page 131).

Marinade:
I large white onion (finely chopped)
2 large tomatoes (finely chopped)
2 cloves garlic (crushed)
1 tablespoon green seasoning (see page 11)
½ teaspoon hot pepper sauce (see page 13)
1 tablespoon salt
1 tablespoon black pepper

Variation 1 Ingredients:
500g/17½oz cod (cubed)
2 tablespoons olive oil
4 tablespoons water
3 tablespoons curry powder
2 teaspoons ground turmeric

Variation 2 Ingredients:
500g/17½oz cod (sliced)
8 tablespoons olive oil
4 tablespoons water
3 tablespoons curry powder
2 teaspoons ground turmeric
64g/2¼oz plain flour
2 medium potatoes (peeled and chopped)

Serves	Preparation	Cooking	Total
4	15/20 min	15/25 min	30/40 min

Place the fish in a large bowl, add the marinade and mix with your hands until all the pieces of fish are evenly coated. Cover the bowl with a lid or cling film. Marinate in the refrigerator for a minimum of 2 hours, or ideally overnight.

Variation 1:
1. Heat the olive oil and 4 tablespoons of water in a large pan over fairly hot heat. Add the curry powder and turmeric, then mix thoroughly with a spoon.
2. Add the marinated fish chunks and cook over medium heat for 5 minutes.
3. Turn the fish gently, reduce the heat and simmer for another 5 minutes or until the fish is tender. Garnish with fresh coriander and serve hot.

Variation 2:
1. Dust the fish slices with flour until they are evenly coated.
2. Heat 6 tablespoons of olive oil in a frying pan over fairly hot heat. Add the fish slices and fry them until they golden brown. Remove from heat and set aside.
3. Heat 2 tablespoons of olive oil and 4 tablespoons of water in a large pan over fairly hot heat. Add the curry powder and turmeric, then mix thoroughly with a spoon.
4. Reduce the heat, add the potatoes to the curry, and simmer for 10 minutes.
5. Add the fried fish and continue to simmer for another 5 minutes. Garnish with fresh coriander and serve hot.

TUNA IN PARSLEY SAUCE

One of the first dishes I learnt as a young man is now a favourite with our children. As delicious as it is quick to make, our Tuna in Parsley Sauce recipe exudes the simplicity, elegance, and style we love in Mediterranean cuisine.

Sauce:
200ml/7oz whole milk
50ml/1¾oz double cream
15g/½oz fresh parsley
(stemmed and chopped)
1 tablespoon plain flour
1 vegetable stock cube
(crushed)
1 teaspoon lemon juice

Other Ingredients:
2 teaspoons olive oil
½ teaspoon garlic
(chopped)
250g/9oz tuna chunks in
spring water (drained)
150g/5¼oz sweetcorn &
peppers (drained)
2 sprigs parsley
(unstemmed for garnish)

Serves	Preparation	Cooking	Total
2	15 min	5 min	20 min

1. Pour all the ingredients for the sauce into a small jug and mix well with a spoon.

2. Sauté the garlic in olive oil, over hot heat, for 1 minute.

3. Reduce the heat to moderate and add the tuna chunks and sweetcorn & peppers. Cook for 1 minute, stirring frequently.

4. Cover the tuna and sweetcorn & peppers with the sauce. Warm for 3 minutes, stirring occasionally, but do not boil.

5. Garnish with parsley sprigs and serve either with conchiglie, fusilli or penne, cooked as recommended by the manufacturer.

COCONUT KING PRAWNS

For a truly tropical culinary experience, our scrumptious Coconut King Prawn recipe is excellent served with Rice & Peas (see page 131). Try it with Tabouleh (see page 117), or as an accompaniment to our Caribbean Chicken Stew (see page 87). Inspired by a recipe from Taste of the Caribbean by Rosamund Grant.

Marinade:
1 tablespoon dark rum
2 teaspoons lime juice
1 teaspoon paprika
1 teaspoon black pepper
1 teaspoon celery salt
1 teaspoon Angostura bitters

Other Ingredients:
36 raw king prawns (peeled, deveined, and washed)
2 tablespoons olive oil
2 cloves garlic (crushed)
I large white onion (finely chopped)
3 tablespoons tomato paste
2 tablespoons fresh coriander (chopped)
1 teaspoon fresh thyme (chopped)
1 teaspoon ground cinnamon
½ teaspoon hot pepper sauce (see page 13)
200g/7oz tinned sweet-corn (drained)
1 tablespoon grated coconut
300ml/10½oz coconut milk

Serves	Preparation	Cooking	Total
4	15 min	20 min	35 min

1. Place the prawns in a large bowl, add the marinade and mix with your hands until all the prawns are evenly coated. Cover the bowl with a lid or cling film. Marinate in the refrigerator for a minimum of 2 hours, or ideally overnight.

2. Using 2 tablespoons of olive oil, sauté the garlic and onion in a saucepan over hot heat for about 2 minutes.

3. Add the marinated prawns and cook until they turn pink. Stir to heat evenly and prevent sticking.

4. Leaving some oil in the saucepan, use a spoon to scoop out the cooked prawns and onion. Put aside in a bowl.

5. Add the tomato paste, coriander, thyme, cinnamon and hot pepper sauce to the saucepan. Stir well, reduce heat and simmer.

6. Pour the sweetcorn, grated coconut, and coconut milk into a food processor and blend until smooth.

7. Pour the blended coconut into the saucepan, stir and continue to simmer until the liquid is reduced.

8. Add the cooked prawns, gently stir, and simmer for about 5 minutes. Salt to taste and serve.

NOTES

NOTES

Salads & Sides

TABOULEH

Originally from the mountains of Lebanon and Syria, tabouleh is a Middle Eastern vegetarian dish that is also an integral part of traditional Armenian cuisine. Tabouleh is a light, delicious, and nutritious side dish made with bulgur, finely chopped parsley, and diced tomatoes seasoned with lemon juice and olive oil.

75g/2¾oz fine bulgur
200g/7oz fresh parsley (stalks removed/finely chopped)
50g/1¾oz fresh mint leaves (finely chopped)
6 medium tomatoes (finely chopped)
10 spring onions (diced into 5mm/¼in widths)
Juice of 1 lemon
2 tablespoons extra virgin olive oil
2 teaspoons salt
2 teaspoons ground black pepper
1 teaspoon paprika or chilli pepper (fresh or ground)

Serves   **Preparation**
  4-6   **30 min**

1. Place the fine bulgur into a bowl then cover it with warm water and leave it to soak for an hour or until it has softened. If you use coarse bulgur, leave it to soak for up to 2 hours or until it has softened. Strain the bulgur thoroughly.
2. Combine the chopped parsley, mint, tomatoes and spring onions in a large bowl.
3. Add the bulgur, lemon juice, and olive oil.
4. Mix in the salt, ground black pepper, and paprika or chilli.
5. Taste to ensure the flavours are well balanced and add further seasoning if needed.
6. Cover the bowl and refrigerate until ready to serve.

Note:
For an authentic tabouleh, only bulgur will do - it cannot be substituted with any other cereal. Bulgur is a whole wheat grain usually sold parboiled and dried. High in fibre and low in fat, bulgur is an ideal ingredient for low-calorie vegetarian or vegan dishes. The highest quality bulgur has uniform particle sizes, which create more consistent cooking results. We recommend fine grain bulgur for tabouleh but coarse bulgur, with its increased cooking time, can also be used for excellent results. Be sure to follow the instructions on the packet.

GRILLED AUBERGINE SALAD

This is a simple and delicious accompaniment to barbecues, grills, and stews. Try it with Armenian Shish Kofte (see page 67) or Lamb & White Bean Stew (see page 77).

3 large purple aubergines
2 red bell peppers (cored and sliced into rings)
2 large tomatoes (sliced)
1 large red onion (sliced into rings)
3 tablespoons parsley (chopped)
2 tablespoons extra virgin olive oil
2 tablespoons lemon juice
Salt and pepper to taste

Serves	Preparation	Cooking	Total
4-6	15 min	30 min	45 min

1. Preheat the oven to 200°C/390°F.

2. Wash the aubergines then pierce their skins a few times with a fork.

3. Cut the aubergines into two pieces, lengthways, then grill them for approximately 30 minutes or until their skins are charred, blackened, and soft when pressed.

4. Using a spoon, scoop out the cooked flesh from each aubergine and cut into small pieces.

5. Place the red bell peppers, tomatoes, onions, grilled aubergine flesh and chopped parsley into a deep bowl and toss.

6. With a large spoon, gently mix in the olive oil, lemon juice, salt and pepper. Refrigerate for 30 minutes, toss, and serve.

ZABOCA & MANGO SALAD

A diet rich in avocados, or zabocas as they are called in Trinidad and Tobago, is known to lower blood cholesterol levels. Our delicious zaboca and mango salad is excellent on its own or with meat, poultry or fish.

5 lettuce leaves
1 large hard mango
1 large hard avocado
1 medium red onion
1 red bell pepper
1 red chilli pepper
2 tablespoons extra virgin olive oil
Juice of 1 lime
Salt and pepper to taste

1. Wash the fruits and vegetables under cold, running water. Cut the lettuce into small strips. Peel and cut the avocado and mango lengthways, into 10mm slices. Cut the onion into 5mm slices and dice the deseeded peppers.
2. Place the lettuce, mango, avocado, onion and pepper into a salad bowl and gently mix together. Be careful not to damage the soft flesh of the avocado and mango.
3. Mix the olive oil, lime juice, salt, pepper and chopped chilli together in a small bowl. Pour over the salad and mix again. Refrigerate for 30 minutes before serving.

SWEET POTATO SALAD

Quick and easy to make; our Sweet Potato Salad can either be a delicious side dish or an excellent vegetarian main meal. Refrigerate before serving, or serve immediately for an interesting combination of warm and cool ingredients.

400g/14oz sweet potatoes (in chunks)
240g/8½oz/1 tin lentils
1 red bell pepper
½ red chilli pepper
15g/½oz chives
4 tablespoons extra virgin olive oil
2 tablespoons white wine vinegar
1 tablespoon lime juice
2 teaspoons honey

1. Preheat the oven to 200°C/390°F. On a baking tray, toss the sweet potatoes with 1 tablespoon of olive oil, and roast for 10 minutes until tender.

2. Wash and rinse the lentils. Place them into a salad bowl and gently mix together with the roasted sweet potatoes, chopped peppers, and chives. Be careful not to damage the soft flesh of the sweet potatoes.

3. Mix the remaining olive oil, vinegar, lime juice and honey together in a small bowl. Pour over the salad and mix again. Season with salt and pepper to taste. Refrigerate for 30 minutes before serving.

TRINIDADIAN POTATO SALAD

For picnics, barbecues, and casual get-togethers, nothing beats a delicious potato salad. A most versatile side dish, our Trinidadian Potato Salad is excellent with Caribbean Chicken Stew (see page 87) and Callaloo (see page 45); or with Grilled Mango Chicken (see page 91) or Rum & Red Peppers Chicken (see page 93).

2 eggs (hard-boiled and diced)
2 teaspoons salt (divided)
400g/14oz potatoes (boiled and cubed)
100g/3½oz green peas (boiled)
100g/3½oz baby carrots (boiled and diced)
20g/¾oz white onion (diced)
20g/¾oz celery (diced)
20g/¾oz red bell pepper (diced)
2 tablespoons mayonnaise
1 teaspoon American mustard
1 teaspoon sweet relish
1 teaspoon paprika (for garnish)

Serves	Preparation	Cooking	Total
4	45 min	15 min	1 hr

1. Place two eggs into a small saucepan with a glass lid. Pour in only enough water to cover the eggs. Place the lid on the pan and bring to the boil over very hot heat. Turn off the heat, and allow the eggs to sit in the hot water for 15 minutes.

2. Meanwhile, peel, wash and cube the potatoes. Place them into a deep pan and boil them in salted water for 8-10 minutes over fairly hot heat. Remove from the heat, transfer to a suitable container and refrigerate.

3. If using tinned or bottled peas and carrots, simply wash with cool running water, drain, then dice the carrots. Cook frozen peas and carrots according to the manufacturer instructions. Remove from the heat, drain, then dice the carrots if necessary. Transfer to a suitable container and refrigerate.

4. Transfer the eggs into a bowl of cold water for 2 minutes. Remove, then peel and dice. Transfer to a suitable container, cover and refrigerate.

5. The eggs, potatoes, peas and carrots should all be cold. Place all the ingredients into a serving bowl and use a spoon to gently mix them together. Try not to crush the potatoes too much as the salad will become mushy. Add salt to taste and garnish with paprika. Serve immediately or cover and store refrigerated no more than 4 days.

JAJUKH

For convenience in reproducing this cool, refreshing Armenian salad, we've substituted matzoon (Armenian fermented milk) with Greek style yogurt.

340g/12oz/2 cucumbers (washed, peeled and diced)
500g/17½oz Greek style yogurt
3 tablespoons fresh mint leaves (finely chopped)
2 tablespoons mint leaves
2 cloves garlic (crushed)
3 teaspoons salt

Serves
4-6

Preparation
15 min

1. Combine the diced cucumber with yogurt in a deep bowl and mix.
2. Add the chopped fresh mint, dried mint, crushed garlic and salt. Mix thoroughly.
3. Taste to ensure the flavours are well balanced and add more salt if required.
4. Cover the bowl and refrigerate.

MIXED BEAN SALAD

This mixed bean salad is an excellent side dish for barbecues, roasts, and stews. Keep refrigerated for up to three days - it only gets better. Perfect with Grilled Mango Chicken (see page 91) or Caribbean Chicken Stew (see page 87).

Salad:

540g/19oz mixed beans (tinned in water)
Note: Drain beans in a colander, wash under cold running tap water, and drain again.
10 spring onions (cut into widths of around 5mm/¼in)

Dressing:

2 tablespoons white wine vinegar
2 tablespoon extra virgin olive oil
2 teaspoons salt and pepper
1 teaspoon chilli pepper (ground or fresh)

1. Combine the salad and dressing in a bowl and mix gently but thoroughly.
2. Taste to ensure flavours are well balanced and add further seasoning and vinegar, if needed.
3. Cover the bowl. Refrigerate for 1 hour before serving.

(Serves 4-6)

PASTA STOCK

A delightfully simple way to infuse pasta with complimentary flavours is by adding various types of stock. A quick and easy recipe for a no-fuss side dish.

1½ stock cubes (of your choice)
400g/14oz pasta
Sauce:
2 tablespoons olive oil
8 tomatoes (chopped)
2 tablespoons ketchup
2 tablespoons thyme
½ stock cube (crushed)
1 tablespoon red wine vinegar

Serves	Preparation	Cooking	Total
4	10 min	10 min	20 min

1. Bring 2 litres/2 quarts of water to boil in a deep pan.
2. Add 1½ stock cubes and stir until dissolved.
3. Add the pasta and cook as recommended.
4. Meanwhile, sauté the tomatoes, ketchup, thyme and crushed stock in olive oil for 3 minutes. Pour in vinegar and simmer for 2 minutes.
5. Drain the pasta and transfer to a serving dish. Mix in the sauce with a spoon and serve.

BAKED MARINATED PULSES

This simple, Mediterranean-style recipe is a quick and delicious alternative to stewed pulses such as lentils, peas, and beans.

Marinade:
2 teaspoons olive oil
1 teaspoon lemon juice
1 teaspoon organic white wine vinegar
2 tomatoes (finely chopped)
½ white onion (finely chopped)
Other Ingredients:
500g/17½oz tinned pulses

Serves	Preparation	Cooking	Total
4	5 min	15 min	20 min

1. Drain the pulses and place in an ovenproof dish. Add the marinade and thoroughly mix with a spoon. Cover the dish with a lid or cling film. Place in the refrigerator and marinate for a minimum of 2 hours, or ideally overnight.
2. Transfer the ovenproof dish to a preheated oven and cook at 180°C/360°F for 25 minutes.
3. Add salt and pepper to taste and serve.

ALMOND & SULTANA PILAF

A delightfully nutty and fruity alternative to plain boiled rice. Great served with meat, poultry, fish or vegetable dishes.

300g/10½oz Basmati rice
40g/1½oz butter (divided)
200ml/7oz chicken or vegetable stock
50g/1¾oz flaked almonds
50g/1¾oz sultanas
½ teaspoon salt
½ teaspoon ground cloves
½ teaspoon ground cinnamon

Serves	Preparation	Cooking	Total
4-6	10 min	30 min	40 min

1. Put the rice in cold, salted water and mix until the water becomes cloudy. Soak for 2 hours, then rinse and sieve under cold, running water.
2. Heat 25g/1oz of butter in a pan, over hot heat, and add the rice. Stir the rice and butter, for a few minutes, until all the rice grains are covered with butter.
3. Add the stock and allow the mixture to begin to boil.
4. Reduce the heat to its lowest setting, cover, and let simmer for 15-20 minutes; or until the stock is absorbed and the rice grains are soft. **Note: you may need to add more stock if the liquid has evaporated but the rice grains have not cooked.**
5. Heat 15g/½oz of butter in a small pan, over hot heat. As the butter melts, add the almonds and sultanas. Stir for a couple of minutes, until the almonds are lightly browned.
6. Add the salt, ground cloves, and cinnamon. Stir for another minute, until all the spices are well mixed with the almonds and sultanas.
7. Transfer the rice to a deep bowl. Pour the spiced almonds and sultanas over the top of the rice, in the middle of the bowl. Alternatively, you can serve the almonds and sultanas thoroughly mixed with the rice, or on a separate plate, thereby allowing diners to sprinkle on the rice to their own liking.

RICE & PEAS

Rice & Peas is a traditional food in the English-speaking Caribbean, which is often, but not exclusively, served with the main Sunday meal. It is made with rice, pigeon peas (also known as gungo peas), cowpeas, or red kidney beans, and compliments many dishes including stewed meat, poultry, fish or seafood.

2 tablespoons olive oil
400g/14oz long grain rice
300ml/10½oz coconut milk
100ml/3½oz water
1 teaspoon allspice
1 stick cinnamon
2 bay leaves (fresh or dried)
salt and black pepper for seasoning
300g/10½oz tinned red kidney beans or pigeon peas (rinsed and drained)

Serves	Preparation	Cooking	Total
4-6	30 min	30 min	1 hr

1. Soak the rice in cold, salted water for 30-45 minutes.

2. Rinse the soaked rice under cold, running tap water then drain.

3. Heat the olive oil in a pan over moderate heat and add the drained rice.

4. Cook for a minute ensuring that the oil covers all the rice grains.

5. Add the water, coconut milk, beans and all the spices and seasoning then bring to the boil.

6. Reduce the heat, cover and simmer gently for about 15 to 20 minutes or until all the liquid is absorbed and the rice is tender. You may need to add more water if all the liquid evaporates but the rice has not softened.

7. Once cooked, fluff with a fork and gently stir before serving.

Note:
Rice & Peas is excellent with Caribbean Chicken Stew (see page 87).

BULGUR PILAF

Serve with meat, poultry or vegetable dishes as an excellent alternative to basmati rice or Rice & Peas (see page 131).

1 tablespoon olive oil
300g/10½oz white bulgur (coarse grain)
200ml/7oz chicken or vegetable stock
1 large onion, (finely chopped)

Serves	Preparation	Cooking	Total
4	5 min	15 min	20 min

1. Fry the onion in the olive oil, in a pan, over moderate heat, until it becomes translucent. Then, stir in the bulgur, coating all the grains with oil.

2. Add the stock and bring to the boil.

3. Reduce the heat to the lowest setting. Cover and let simmer for 10-15 minutes, or until all the stock is absorbed and the grains are soft. Add more stock if the liquid has evaporated but the bulgur is not cooked.

133

OKRA STEW

Variations of okra stews exist in Armenian, Anatolian, Middle Eastern, African, Indian, Caribbean and Mediterranean cuisines. Our stew recipe for bamya, bhindi, okra, ochro, lady's fingers, gumbo or whatever you call it is versatile, scrumptious, and rich in vitamins C and K. It is a great vegetarian dish, either as a main course, served with Bulgur Pilaf (see page 133) or as a side dish.

2 tablespoons olive oil
I large white onion (finely chopped)
300g/10½oz fresh or frozen baby okras
(washed with stems and tips trimmed)
1 tablespoon tomato paste
450g/16oz/1 tin chopped tomatoes
1 clove garlic (crushed)
1 teaspoon cumin
1 teaspoon coriander
1 teaspoon paprika
Salt and pepper for seasoning

Serves	Preparation	Cooking	Total
4-6	10 min	50 min	1 hr

1. Heat the olive oil in a large pan over fairly hot heat.

2. Stir in the chopped onion and cook until soft but not browned.

3. Add the okra and tomato paste. Sauté for a few minutes.

4. Ensuring the okra is not shredded, gently stir in the chopped tomatoes, crushed garlic, and spices. Add salt and pepper to taste and stir again. Reduce the heat, cover the pan and simmer for 45 minutes or until the okra is very tender but not shredded.

Note: You can substitute the okra with green beans, white beans, courgettes, aubergines or your favourite vegetable.

GARLIC & CHILLI MELONGENE

The aubergine in British English is known by several names - badinjan among Armenians, eggplant in the USA, melongene by Trinidad & Tobago's African descendants and baigan by those of Indian heritage. Superb with Caribbean Chicken Stew (see page 87) and Rice & Peas (see page 131). Inspired by a recipe from Taste of the Caribbean by Rosamund Grant.

2 tablespoons olive oil
2 cloves garlic (crushed)
3 large tomatoes (peeled and chopped)
2 tablespoons red pepper paste (see page 15)
4 large aubergines (top discarded and chopped into 25mm/1in cubes)
150ml/5¼oz vegetable stock
5 tablespoons spring onions (chopped)
1 red bell pepper (chopped into 25mm/1in cubes)
1 hot chilli pepper (finely chopped)
½ teaspoon ground black pepper
½ teaspoon salt
3 tablespoons lemon juice
2 tablespoons fresh chopped coriander (divided)
2 teaspoons Angostura bitters

Serves	Preparation	Cooking	Total
4-6	10 min	20 min	30 min

1. Heat the olive oil in a large frying pan on medium heat then add the garlic, tomatoes, and red pepper paste. Stir-fry for 2 minutes or until slightly softened.

2. Mix in the aubergines, add the stock and cover the pan. Reduce the heat and simmer until the aubergines are soft and tender.

3. Mix in the spring onions.

4. Gently stir in the red bell pepper, hot chilli pepper, and ground black pepper. Add salt to taste and continue to stir until all the vegetables are thoroughly mixed.

5. Add the rum and lemon juice, cover and simmer for another 3-5 minutes or until the aubergines and red bell pepper are soft (but not too soft).

6. Stir in 1½ tablespoons coriander and simmer for another 2 minutes. Remove the frying pan from the heat, gently stir in the Angostura bitters, and garnish with the remaining coriander.

VOSPOV KUFTEH

Vospov Kufteh or Lentil Patty is a traditional Armenian dish made with red lentils and fine bulgur or dried, cracked wheat. Don't let its 'washday' simplicity lower your expectations; this delicious, healthy recipe is an excellent choice for vegetarians, either as a main course or as a starter with Tabouleh (see page 117).

1 tablespoon olive oil
200g/7oz dried red lentils (rinsed and drained)
100g/3½oz bulgur (must be fine grain)
1 large red bell pepper (finely diced)
1 large white onion (finely chopped)
1 tablespoon flat parsley (finely chopped)
2 tablespoons spring onions (chopped)
200ml/7oz water
1 teaspoon paprika
1 teaspoon salt
Note:
In Armenia, Vospov Kufteh is also known as 'washday food'.
In days of old, before the advent of automatic washing machines, Armenian housewives could easily spend an entire day doing the week's washing by hand. With no time to cook elaborate meals, Vospov Kufteh became their 'washday food' of choice.

Serves	Preparation	Cooking	Total
4-6	10 min	30 min	40 min

1. Combine the lentils and water in a large pan and bring to the boil over high heat.

2. Reduce the heat to low, cover and simmer for 30 minutes or until the lentils are tender and most of the water is absorbed.

3. Stir in the bulgur and salt to taste. Remove from the heat and let stand for 20 minutes, allowing the bulgur to absorb all the liquid.

4. Meanwhile, heat the olive oil over medium heat in a small pan. Add the chopped onion and cook, stirring frequently until it is soft and golden. Remove from the heat and leave to cool for 5 minutes.

5. Combine the cooked onions with the bulgur and lentils mixture. Stir in the chopped spring onions, bell pepper, and parsley then leave to cool.

6. With clean hands moistened with water, knead the mixture in a bowl until it is thoroughly blended. Add small amounts of water as required to keep the mixture moist. Salt to taste.

7. Form the mixture into 2-inch patties. Arrange them on a serving dish and sprinkle with paprika powder.

NOTES

NOTES

Desserts

BOOZY FRUIT CUPCAKES

Our Caribbean-style Boozy Fruit Cupcakes are a delightful alternative to mince pies. Serve with Rum & Raisin Ice Cream (see page 167) and an ice cold glass of Trinidadian Sorrel (see page 197).

Filling:
30g/1oz prunes (pitted)
30g/1oz raisins
30g/1oz currants
30g/1oz mixed candied citrus peel
30g/1oz flaked almonds
100ml/3½oz rum
100ml/3½oz brandy
1 teaspoon ground nutmeg
1 teaspoon mixed spice
1 teaspoon ground cinnamon
½ teaspoon Angostura bitters

Cupcake:
100g/3½oz unsalted butter (room temperature)
100g/3½oz brown sugar
2 eggs (room temperature)
1 teaspoon vanilla extract
1 teaspoon almond extract
100g/3½oz plain flour
1 teaspoon baking powder

Serves	Preparation	Cooking	Total
20	15 min	15 min	30 min

1. Place the filling ingredients into an airtight container or hermetically sealed jar. Mix well and set aside in a dark place, at room temperature, for 2 hours or longer.

2. Preheat the oven to 190°C/370°F and place the cupcake cases into cupcake baking trays.

3. Transfer the filling mixture to a food processor and mince into a textured paste. Remove and set aside.

4. Use the food processor to blend the butter and sugar together until creamy in texture.

5. Mix in the eggs, vanilla extract, and almond extract then add the flour and baking powder and blend again.

6. Add the filling mixture and mix well with a spoon.

7. Spoon the mixture into individual cupcake cases and bake for 15 minutes in the centre of the oven. **Note: Do not open the oven for the first 10 minutes of baking. To check if the cupcakes are properly baked, insert a toothpick into each cupcake. When removed, the toothpick should be clean with no cupcake mixture attached to it. If any of the cupcake mixture adheres to the toothpick, return the cupcake to the oven and continue baking. Check the cupcakes every minute with the toothpick until they are properly baked.**

8. Remove the cupcakes from the oven and leave them to cool for 15-20 minutes. Serve immediately or transfer them to an airtight storage container. **Optional: dust the cupcakes with icing sugar before serving.**

(Makes 20 cupcakes)

ALMOND BERRY CAKE

Our Almond Berry Cake recipe combines glacé cherries, sherry-laced cranberries, and ground almonds flavoured with amaretto, mulberry syrup, and cinnamon. Serve with a scoop of Custard Ice Cream (see page 163) or Vanilla Ice Cream (see page 165) and a cup of Armenian Style Coffee (see page 207) or Earl Grey tea.

Fruit Filling:
100g/3½oz dried cranberries
100g/3½oz glacé cherries
2 tablespoons sherry

Flavouring:
100g/3½oz ground almonds
6 teaspoons mulberry syrup
2 teaspoons amaretto
1 teaspoon ground cinnamon
1 teaspoon almond extract

Cake:
140g/5oz unsalted butter
140g/5oz caster sugar
2 medium eggs
140g/5oz self-raising flour

Dusting:
Icing sugar

Garnish:
Glacé cherries

Serves	Preparation	Cooking	Total
10	20 min	25 min	45 min

1. Place the filling ingredients into an airtight container or hermetically sealed jar. Mix well and set aside in a dark place, at room temperature, for 2 hours or longer.

2. Preheat the oven to 180°C/360°F. Grease and flour a 20cm/8in square baking tin.

3. Use a blender or food processor to blend the flavouring ingredients together with the butter and sugar for 1 minute. Use a spatula to scrape down any mixture adhering to the sides of the bowl then continue to blend for another minute until smooth and creamy.

4. Mix in the eggs, one at a time, then add the flour and blend for 1 minute, until no flour is visible.

5. Pour the fruit filling into the mixing bowl and pulse for 2 seconds.

6. Spoon the cake mixture into the baking tin and use the spatula to smooth the surface. Bake for 25 minutes in the centre of the oven. Check with a toothpick. **Note: Be careful not to burn the top of the cake. If it begins to brown too quickly, cover the top with foil.**

7. Remove the cake from the oven and leave it to cool for 15-20 minutes. Dust with icing sugar, slice and serve.

CURRANTS ROLL

The Trinidad and Tobago currants roll is a popular, traditional, flaky pastry dessert, based on the British Eccles cake, created in the late 18th century. The addition of rum and bitters makes our recipe quite moist. For a drier, more traditional currants roll, simply omit our optional ingredients for the filling.

Puff pastry:
1½ cups plain flour
¼ teaspoon salt
½ cup ice cold water
80g/3oz cold unsalted butter

Or:
Ready-made puff pastry

Filling:
1 cup currants
¼ cup brown sugar
1 teaspoon dark rum (optional)
2 teaspoons ground nutmeg
½ teaspoon vanilla extract (optional)
½ teaspoon cinnamon
1 dash Angostura bitters (optional)

Glaze (optional):
1 egg (beaten)
1 tablespoon milk
1 teaspoon dark rum
1 dash Angostura bitters

Serves	Preparation	Cooking	Total
4-6	1 hr	30 min	1 hr 30 min

1. Place the flour into a mixing bowl. Mix in the salt, add ice cold water and quickly knead into a ball of dough.

2. Cover the dough with cling film or place into a freezer bag and seal without trapping any air. Place the dough in a freezer drawer for 7 minutes.

3. While waiting, use a suitable container to mix the filling ingredients together. Refrigerate until needed.

4. Place the solid butter between two sheets of waxed paper and flatten into a rectangle using a rolling pin. Refrigerate until needed.

5. Place the dough on a flat, floured surface and flatten into a thin rectangle. Carefully wrap the flattened butter with the dough.

6. Using the rolling pin, and ensuring the butter does not seep out, carefully flatten the butter wrapped in dough into a thin rectangle. Fold the rectangle, wrap it with cling film and place it in a freezer drawer for 15 minutes. Repeat this flattening, folding and then placing into the freezer drawer, two more times.

7. Pre-heat the oven to 200°C/390°F and line a baking tray with baking parchment. Set aside the mixed glaze.

8. Using the rolling pin, flatten the dough into a rectangle one last time. **Note: your finished currants roll will be as long as the short side of the rectangular dough.** Spread the filling evenly on the surface of the rectangular dough, then carefully roll it.

9. Place the roll on the baking tray. Brush on the glaze, and bake for 20-30 minutes until lightly browned. Once baked, let cool for 30 minutes before slicing diagonally.

APRICOT & PISTACHIO CRUMBLE

The crumble is a dish of British origin, however, our recipe calls for apricots and pistachio nuts, which are popular ingredients in Armenia and the Middle East. Serve warm with ice cream for a gorgeous, mouth-watering, spicy delight that combines the warm with the cold; and the sweet, smoothness of the apricots with the subtly salted crunch of the pistachios.

240g/8½oz tinned apricots (drained and cut in half)
90g/3¼oz plain flour
50g/1¾oz unsalted butter (cubed)
40g/1½oz pistachios (shelled and chopped)
30g/1oz soft brown sugar
2 teaspoons ground nutmeg
2 teaspoons mixed spice

Serves	Preparation	Cooking	Total
4	10 min	25 min	35 min

1. Preheat the oven to 180°C/360°F.

2. Place the apricots into a shallow, buttered, ovenproof dish and sprinkle with 1 teaspoon of mixed spice and 1 teaspoon of ground nutmeg.

3. Sift the flour into a large bowl and mix together with the sugar. Use your fingertips to rub the cubes of butter into the mixture until it resembles coarse breadcrumbs.

4. Add the pistachios, ground nutmeg, and mixed spice. Mix all the ingredients of the crumble together with a spoon.

5. Sprinkle the crumble all over the apricots coating them well.

6. Place the dish on the centre shelf of the oven and bake for about 25 minutes, or until the apricots are cooked and the top of the crumble has browned.

7. Serve warm with Apricot Ice Cream (see page 169), Custard Ice Cream (see page 163), or Vanilla Ice Cream (see page 165).

BLACK CAKE

Trinidadian Black Cake is a rum cake, which is traditionally made during the Christmas season with dried fruits that have been soaked in rum and cherry brandy for several days or months. Large jars, filled with boozy fruit, stored in dark kitchen cupboards are commonplace in Trinidad and Tobago. Trinidadians often make four large cakes at a time; however, our recipe is for just one cake.

Serves	Preparation	Cooking	Total
12-16	20 min	3 hrs	3 hrs 20 min

Fruit Base:
250g/9oz prunes (pitted)
250g/9oz currants
150g/5¼oz raisins
100g/3½oz sultanas
40g/1½oz glacé cherries
20g/¾oz mixed peel
200ml brandy
100ml dark rum (add more if you like)
2 tablespoons sherry
2 teaspoons Angostura bitters

Browning:
250g burnt sugar syrup (see page 21)

Cake:
250g unsalted butter
250g soft brown sugar
2 large eggs
2 teaspoons lime juice
1 teaspoon vanilla extract
1 teaspoon almond extract
250g plain flour
1 teaspoon baking powder
1 teaspoon mixed spice
1 teaspoon nutmeg

Glaze:
250ml rum or sherry (add more if you like)

Fruit Base:
Use a food processor to mix all the fruit base ingredients together into a coarse purée. Transfer the fruit purée into a sealed, airtight container and leave it to soak at room temperature for a minimum of 2 hours, or ideally overnight. It is not necessary to soak the fruit for days, months or years, but don't let us stop you.

Browning:
Make the browning, multiplying the ingredients on page 21 by 5 to make 250g of burnt sugar syrup.

Cake:
1. Preheat the oven to 140°C/280°F.
2. Using a food processor, cream the butter and sugar then add the eggs one at a time and continue mixing.
3. Mix in the lime juice and extracts of vanilla and almond.
4. Mix in the flour, baking powder, mixed spice and nutmeg.
5. Mix in the fruit purée and browning.
6. Pour the cake mixture into a large tin lined with parchment or a festive silicone mould greased with butter.
7. Bake the cake for 3 hours. Use a toothpick to ensure that it is properly baked.
8. Remove the cake from the oven and place it on a large plate, tray or cake stand. Using a toothpick, pierce the cake in several places, while it is still hot. Gradually pour the glaze over the cake and leave it to cool. Brush on more glaze, as necessary, to prevent the cake from drying. **Note: this cake can cause intoxication.**

CHRISTMAS CRACKERS

With exotic Middle Eastern and traditional fruit fillings, our Christmas Crackers recipes are a perfect addition to any festive meal. Serve warm with Custard Ice Cream (see page 163) or Vanilla Ice Cream (see page 165).

10 chilled phyllo (filo) sheets 480mm x 255mm (19in x 10in)
20g/¾oz butter (melted)

Middle Eastern Filling:
80g/2¾oz pine nuts
44g/1½oz fresh apples (peeled and diced)
32g/1oz dried soft apricots (diced)
32g/1oz dried dates (diced)
32g/1oz dried figs (diced)
32g/1oz sultanas
32g/1oz of dried soft prunes (pitted and diced)
½ teaspoon ground cinnamon
50ml/1¾oz brandy
32g/1oz sponge fingers (finely crumbled)

Traditional Filling:
See page 161

Ties:
see page 161

Icing sugar or powdered sugar (for dusting)

Serves	Preparation	Cooking	Total
5	10 min	15 min	25 min

1. Place all the Middle Eastern filling ingredients, except the sponge fingers, into a deep pot and bring to the boil over hot heat. Reduce the heat to simmer for 2 more minutes, stirring frequently. Remove from the heat, and leave to cool. Mix, cover, and refrigerate for at least 4 hours or preferably overnight. Mix in the sponge fingers. Repeat this procedure for the traditional filling ingredients (see page 161).

2. Remove 2 phyllo sheets at a time from the pack, and keep the unused sheets covered with a damp kitchen towel.

3. Lay the phyllo sheets flat on a clean work surface and cut them into half (9.5 x 5 inches).

4. Each cracker will have two layers of phyllo sheets. Brush one phyllo sheet with melted butter, then stack another sheet on top of it and brush it with melted butter.

5. Place the filling in the middle of the stacked pastry sheets then roll up the pastry lengthways into a tube. To create a cracker, pinch the pastry ends, tie them with strips of apricot, and crimp the edges. Place the crackers on a buttered oven tray and brush them all over with melted butter, not forgetting their crimped edges.

6. Repeat this process to prepare a total of 4 Middle Eastern crackers and 1 traditional cracker.

Continued on page 161.

160

CHRISTMAS CRACKERS

Continued from page 159.

Traditional Filling:
30g/1oz dried cranberries
20g/¾oz pine nuts
½ teaspoon ground nutmeg
10ml/¼oz brandy
6g/¼oz/1 sponge finger (finely crumbled)

Ties:
Dried apricots (cut into thin strips)

Serves	Preparation	Cooking	Total
5	10 min	15 min	25 min

7. Preheat the oven to 200°C/390°F.
8. Bake the crackers for 15 minutes, or until the pastry is golden and crisp. Be careful not to burn the pastry.
9. Transfer the Christmas crackers to a serving dish and dust with icing sugar or powdered sugar.

Note:
Our Christmas Crackers are an excellent alternative to the traditional Christmas pudding that can be made in advance and stored in the freezer. However, do not brush the pastry with butter before freezing. You can place them straight into a pre-heated oven from frozen, adding melted butter on top.

Tip:
Be creative, and have fun experimenting. How about trying some dried Caribbean fruits with rum? Substitute the apples with pears, or combine different fresh or dried ingredients with the boozy marinade of your choice.

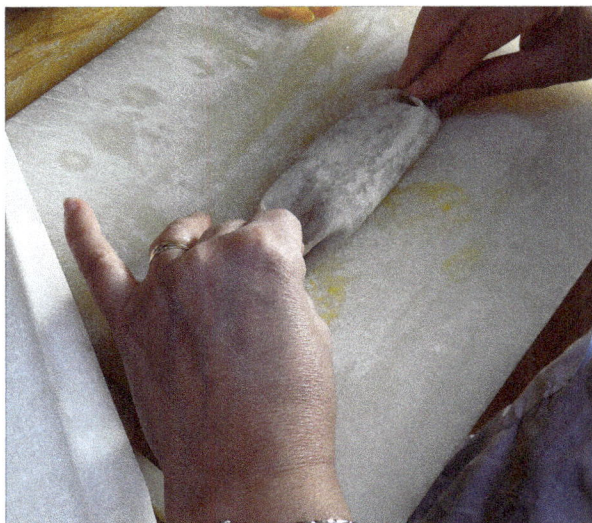

CUSTARD ICE CREAM

This recipe is inspired by the basic, most popular type of homemade ice cream in Trinidad and Tobago. If used, eggs should be cooked at an internal temperature of 70°C/160°F to destroy Salmonella, if present. To make our ice creams and sorbets we use a counter-top, electric ice cream maker with a pre-frozen bowl. Enjoy!

340g/12oz evaporated milk
2 medium free-range egg yolks
400g/14oz custard
400g/14oz condensed milk
1 teaspoon vanilla extract
1 dash Angostura bitters

Note: If you are in a hurry or you prefer a softer ice cream, all our ice cream recipes can be made without eggs. Simply ensure that all the ingredients are properly chilled and churn for 30 minutes.

Yield
2L/67½oz

1. Freeze the freezer bowl of the ice-cream maker following the manufacturer's instructions.
2. Pour the evaporated milk into a medium pan and heat over moderate heat for about 5 minutes or until fine bubbles begin to form. Do not boil the milk. Remove from the heat and set aside for 10 minutes.
3. Whisk the egg yolks in a mixing bowl then stir in 2 tablespoons of hot milk.
4. Gently heat the evaporated milk over a low heat setting. Pour in the whisked egg yolks, stirring constantly until the mixture begins to thicken. Using a cooking thermometer, heat the mixture for about 10 minutes until it reaches 70°C/160°F. Remove from the heat, whisk, and strain into a cold saucepan. Set aside to cool.
5. Stir in the custard, condensed milk, vanilla extract and Angostura bitters. Mix, cover, and refrigerate for at least 4 hours, until the mixture is cold, or preferably overnight.
6. Following the manufacturer's instructions, churn the mixture in the ice-cream maker for about 30 minutes.
7. Once churned, the ice cream can be served. However, we prefer to transfer the ice cream into an air-tight, freezer-proof container and freeze overnight.
8. To allow the ice cream to soften a little, remove it from the freezer 5 minutes before serving.

VANILLA ICE CREAM

First used among the Mesoamerican Aztec people of central Mexico, vanilla was brought to Spain by conquistadors in the 1500s. From Spain, its use in foods and drinks spread to the rest of Europe, including France, where French vanilla ice cream was created. Considered by some to be the basic ice cream flavour, vanilla's popularity still reigns supreme.

330ml/11½oz whole milk
250g/9oz granulated sugar
650ml/23oz double cream
2 teaspoons vanilla extract
1 dash Angostura bitters
1 Madagascan vanilla pod

Note: All of our ice cream recipes can be made without eggs. However, if you prefer a richer, harder ice cream, simply add custard made with the yolks of 2 free range eggs, and whole milk instead of evaporated milk (see page 163, steps 3 & 4). Ensure that all the ingredients are properly chilled and churn for 30 minutes.

Yield
2L/67½oz

1. Freeze the freezer bowl of the ice-cream maker following the manufacturer's instructions.

2. Pour the milk and sugar into a food processor or blender and thoroughly blend until the sugar dissolves. Stir in the double cream, vanilla extract, and Angostura bitters.

3. Open the Madagascan vanilla pod, scrape out the seeds into the ice-cream mixture, and pulse for 10 seconds.

4. Transfer the mixture to a suitable container and add the whole vanilla pod. Mix with a spoon, cover, and refrigerate for at least 4 hours or preferably overnight.

5. Remove the Madagascan vanilla pod.

6. Following the manufacturer's instructions, churn the mixture in the ice-cream maker for about 30 minutes.

7. Once churned, the ice cream can be served. However, we prefer to transfer the ice cream into an air-tight, freezer-proof container and freeze overnight.

8. To allow the ice cream to soften a little, remove 5 minutes before serving.

RUM & RAISIN ICE CREAM

Strictly speaking, our Rum & Raisin Ice Cream is technically rum and sultanas ice cream. We prefer the juicy taste of sultanas for our recipe. However, feel free to substitute the sultanas with raisins if you so desire. Smooth, fruity, and with a hint of nuttiness, our Rum & Raisin Ice Cream is to die for.

200ml/7oz dark rum
250g/9oz sultanas
½ teaspoon ground nutmeg
½ teaspoon almond extract
300ml/10½oz whole milk
200g/7oz granulated sugar
600ml/21oz double cream
30g/1oz Agave nectar
2 teaspoons vanilla extract

Note: All of our ice cream recipes can be made without eggs. However, if you prefer a richer, harder ice cream, simply add custard made with the yolks of 2 free range eggs, and whole milk instead of evaporated milk (see page 163, steps 3 & 4). Ensure that all the ingredients are properly chilled and churn for 30 minutes.

Yield
2L/67½oz

1. Freeze the freezer bowl of the ice-cream maker following the manufacturer's instructions.

2. Place the rum, sultanas, ground nutmeg and almond extract into a deep pot and bring to the boil over hot heat. Reduce the heat to simmer for 2 more minutes, stirring frequently. Remove from the heat, and leave to cool. Mix, cover, and refrigerate for at least 4 hours or preferably overnight.

3. Pour the milk and sugar into a food processor or blender and thoroughly blend until the sugar dissolves. Stir in the double cream, Agave nectar and vanilla extract. Pulse for 10 seconds.

4. Transfer the mixture to a suitable container and add the rum-soaked sultanas. Mix with a spoon, cover, and refrigerate for at least 4 hours or preferably overnight.

5. Following the manufacturer's instructions, churn the mixture in the ice-cream maker for about 30 minutes.

6. Once churned, the ice cream can be served. However, we prefer to transfer the ice cream into an air-tight, freezer-proof container and freeze overnight.

APRICOT ICE CREAM

Bristling with health-enhancing properties, the apricot is an excellent choice for fruit desserts. Our apricot ice cream is sweet, spicy, and nutty. However, you can omit the cardamom or just the pistachio nuts or both, to make an equally delicious, silky-smooth, full-flavoured ice cream. This ice cream is excellent on its own or served with our lovely Apricot & Pistachio Crumble (see page 155).

960g/34oz tinned apricots
250g/9oz granulated sugar (divided)
2 tablespoons lemon juice
600ml/21¼oz double cream
300ml/10½oz whole milk
50g/1¾oz pistachio nuts (coarsely crushed)
Seeds from 4 cardamom pods (finely powdered)
Crack open the pods and grind the seeds using a spice grinder.
Note: if using a manual grinder, sieve the seeds to extract only the fine powder.

**Yield
2L/67½oz**

1. Freeze the freezer bowl of the ice-cream maker following the manufacturer's instructions.

2. Place the apricots, 100g of sugar, and lemon juice into a medium saucepan over medium heat. Cook for 30 minutes until the apricots have completely softened. Leave to cool.

4. Purée the apricot mixture using a food processor or blender. Add the cream, whole milk, remaining sugar, and cardamom powder. Blend thoroughly.

5. Transfer the mixture to a suitable container. Mix with a spoon, cover, and refrigerate for at least 4 hours or preferably overnight.

6. Following the manufacturer's instructions, churn the mixture in the ice-cream maker for about 30 minutes. Add the crushed pistachios during the last 10 minutes of churning.

7. Once churned, the ice cream can be served. However, we prefer to transfer the ice cream into an air-tight, freezer-proof container and freeze overnight.

8. To allow the ice cream to soften a little, remove 5 minutes before serving.

COCONUT ICE CREAM

For me, Coconut Ice Cream brings back wonderful childhood memories of hand-cranked wooden churns and noisy, primitive, electric ice cream makers. For most of us, ice cream is simply one of life's purest and most innocent pleasures. Enjoy our dreamy, Trinidadian style Coconut Ice Cream recipe on its own or with a fruit cocktail or fruit salad.

340g/12oz evaporated milk
2 medium free-range egg yolks (optional)
400g/14oz coconut milk
400g/14oz condensed milk
100g/3½oz custard
2 tablespoons grated coconut (optional)
1 teaspoon vanilla extract
1 dash Angostura bitters
Maraschino cherries (optional garnish)

Note: If you are in a hurry or you prefer a softer ice cream, all our ice cream recipes can be made without eggs. Simply ensure that all the ingredients are properly chilled and churn for 30 minutes.

Yield
2L/67½oz

1. Freeze the freezer bowl of the ice-cream maker following the manufacturer's instructions.
2. Pour the evaporated milk into a medium pan and heat over moderate heat for about 5 minutes or until fine bubbles begin to form. Do not boil the milk. Remove from the heat and set aside for 10 minutes.
3. Whisk the egg yolks in a mixing bowl then stir in 2 tablespoons of hot milk.
4. Gently heat the evaporated milk over a low heat setting. Pour in the whisked egg yolks, stirring constantly until the mixture begins to thicken. Using a cooking thermometer, heat the mixture for about 10 minutes until it reaches 70°C/160°F. Remove from the heat, whisk, and strain into a cold saucepan. Set aside to cool.
5. Stir in the coconut milk, condensed milk, custard, grated coconut, vanilla extract and Angostura bitters. Mix, cover, and refrigerate for at least 4 hours, until the mixture is cold, or preferably overnight.
6. Following the manufacturer's instructions, churn the mixture in the ice-cream maker for about 30 minutes.
7. Once churned, the ice cream can be served. However, we prefer to transfer the ice cream into an air-tight, freezer-proof container and freeze overnight.
8. To allow the ice cream to soften a little, remove it from the freezer 5 minutes before serving.

POMEGRANATE SORBET

The pomegranate has been cultivated in the Middle East since ancient times and is reputed to have several health benefits. Be that as it may, our easy to make sorbet is a sweet, delightful indulgence.

900ml/31½oz pomegranate juice.
150ml/5¼oz boiling water
150g/5¼oz caster sugar
50ml/3½oz golden syrup
2 tablespoons lemon juice
1 tablespoon white rum
½ teaspoon salt
½ teaspoon gelatine (or vegetarian gelling powder)

Optional:
1 sprig of mint leaves
Pomegranate seeds (for topping)

Yield
1½L/50¾oz

1. Freeze the freezer bowl of the ice-cream maker following the manufacturer's instructions.
2. Place the sugar into a deep pan, add boiling water and stir until the sugar completely dissolves.
3. Add the pomegranate juice, lemon juice, white rum and golden syrup then briskly stir everything together. Let cool and add salt to taste.
4. Place a cup of the cool sorbet mixture into a small pan. Sprinkle the gelatine granules into it, stir and let stand for 10 minutes. Heat gently over moderate heat, stirring continuously until the gelatine is dissolved. Then, mix it into the sorbet mixture.
5. Cover and refrigerate overnight or for a minimum of 6 hours until the mixture is cold.
6. Following the manufacturer's instructions, churn the mixture in the ice-cream maker for about 30 minutes.
7. Once churned, the sorbet can be served. However, for better results, pour into an air-tight, freezer-proof container and freeze for one hour.
8. To allow the sorbet to soften a little, remove 5 minutes before serving.
9. Top with sprinkled pomegranate seeds, garnish with a sprig of mint and serve.

PASSIONFRUIT SORBET

Also known as maracuya, granadille, maracujá and liliko'i, passionfruit is a vine species of passion flower, native to southern Brazil, Paraguay and northern Argentina. For our refreshing passionfruit sorbet, we use ready-made juice. You can use freshly squeezed passionfruit juice but remember to add at least 50 grammes of caster sugar.

900ml/31½oz passionfruit juice
150ml/5¼oz boiling water
150g/5¼oz glucose
2 tablespoons lemon juice
½ teaspoon salt
1 teaspoon gelatine (or vegetarian gelling powder)
1 teaspoon Angostura bitters

Yield
1½L/50¾oz

1. Freeze the freezer bowl of the ice-cream maker following the manufacturer's instructions.

2. Place the glucose into a deep pan, add boiling water and stir until the glucose completely dissolves.

3. Shake or stir the passionfruit juice before adding it to the glucose syrup. Add the lemon juice then briskly stir everything together. Let cool and add salt to taste.

4. Place a cup of the cool sorbet mixture into a small pan. Sprinkle the gelatine granules into it, stir and let stand for 10 minutes. Heat gently over moderate heat, stirring continuously until the gelatine is dissolved. Then, mix it into the sorbet mixture.

5. Stir in the Angostura bitters, cover and refrigerate overnight or for a minimum of 6 hours until the mixture is cold.

6. Following the manufacturer's instructions, churn the mixture in the ice-cream maker for about 30 minutes.

7. Once churned, the sorbet can be served. However, for better results, pour into an air-tight, freezer-proof container and freeze for one hour.

8. To allow the sorbet to soften a little, remove 5 minutes before serving.

SORREL SORBET

Our delicious sorrel sorbet is made using unsweetened sorrel. For the flavour, follow our Trinidadian Sorrel recipe (see page 197) but do not add sugar. Since sorrel is seasonal, sorrel drinks and liqueurs are usually made as part of traditional Caribbean Christmas festivities. And, in colder climes, sorrel can be an excellent alternative to mulled wine.

650ml/23oz unsweetened sorrel drink
400ml/14oz boiling water
200g/7oz caster sugar
100g/3½oz glucose
2 tablespoons lemon juice
½ teaspoon salt
1 teaspoon gelatine (or vegetarian gelling powder)
1 teaspoon Angostura bitters

Yield
1½L/50¾oz

1. Freeze the freezer bowl of the ice-cream maker following the manufacturer's instructions.

2. Place the sugar and glucose into a deep pan, add boiling water and stir until completely dissolved.

3. Strain the sorrel drink into the pan, pour in the lemon juice and briskly stir everything together. Let cool and add salt to taste.

4. Place a cup of the cool sorbet mixture into a small pan. Sprinkle the gelatine granules into it, stir and let stand for 10 minutes. Heat gently over moderate heat, stirring continuously until the gelatine is dissolved. Then, mix it into the sorbet mixture.

5. Stir in the Angostura bitters, cover and refrigerate overnight or for a minimum of 6 hours until the mixture is cold.

6. Following the manufacturer's instructions, churn the mixture in the ice-cream maker for about 30 minutes.

7. Once churned, the sorbet can be served. However, for better results, pour into an air-tight, freezer-proof container and freeze for one hour.

8. To allow the sorbet to soften a little, remove 5 minutes before serving.

NOTES

NOTES

Drinks

WAYNE'S MAI TAI

Nothing evokes blissful memories of hot, exotic summer destinations better than a great cocktail. And, this is a great cocktail. However, don't be misled by its sweet pineapple juice and sugarcane syrup. Wayne's Mai Tai has hidden strength. So, prepare to enter a state of deeper relaxation. Best shaken, not stirred, with generous amounts of crushed ice.

112ml/4oz pineapple juice
28ml/1oz dark rum
28ml/1oz white rum
28ml/1oz sugarcane syrup
14ml/½oz Curaçao (liqueur)
14ml/½oz Cointreau
14ml/½oz lime juice
7ml/¼oz grenadine
1 dash Angostura bitters
(Serves 4)

Or:
8 parts pineapple juice
2 parts dark rum
2 parts white rum
2 parts sugarcane syrup
1 part Curaçao (liqueur)
1 part Cointreau
1 part lime juice
½ part grenadine
1 dash Angostura bitters

1. Pour all the ingredients into a shaker with ice and shake vigorously for 17 seconds.

2. Strain into a highball glass half filled with crushed ice.

3. Garnish with an orange slice and a sprig of mint, or a pineapple wedge and a maraschino cherry.

4. Serve with a straw to a responsible adult who has no intentions whatsoever of driving or operating heavy machinery within the next 12 hours.

RUM & RED PEPPERS

This infusion combines two of the most distinctive ingredients in our recipes: Caribbean dark rum and the red bell pepper- a match made in heaven.

600ml/21oz dark rum
2 red bell peppers
(washed)

Note:
Make as much as you like, allowing 1 medium red bell pepper for every 300ml/11oz dark rum.

1. With a sharp knife, cut off the tops of the bell peppers then scoop out the seeds and innards. Cut each pepper in half, carefully trim away any remaining innards, and cut into lengthwise slices.
2. Place the slices into a sterile 1L/1qt/2pt Hermetic storage jar.
3. Pour in the rum.
4. Refrigerate for a minimum of 24 hours.
5. Strain and serve over crushed ice garnished with one of the pepper slices or a lemon wedge.
Note: can be substituted for dark rum in our recipes.

CUBA ROJA

Our variation of the famous Cuba Libre calls for Rum & Red Peppers (see page 187).

1 part Rum & Red
Peppers (liquid)
2 parts cola
1 slice red bell pepper
(from Rum & Red
Peppers)
Cubed ice

1. Fill half of a lowball glass with ice.

2. Pour in the Rum & Red Pepper liquid, add the cola and stir gently.

3. Drop in one slice of red bell pepper from your Rum & Red Peppers infusion.

MAUBY

Sweet with a mildly bitter aftertaste, mauby is a traditional, tree-bark based beverage made in the Caribbean. Family recipes and regional variations are often handed down from one generation to the next. Serve ice cold.

5 mauby bark pieces
3 bay leaves
1 cinnamon stick
6 cloves
1 teaspoon fennel seeds or anise seeds
For the mauby drink:
Cola essence
Mixed essence
Angostura bitters
Granulated sugar

Bring the washed ingredients and 700ml/24½oz of water to boil in a saucepan. Reduce the heat and simmer for 30 minutes. Cool and strain into a sterile Hermetic jar and refrigerate. **Note: this mixture will be bitter and it must be diluted and sweetened to taste.**

To make the mauby drink:
Pour 100ml/3½oz mauby mixture and 1L/1qt cold water into a suitable jug. Stir in 2 dashes of Angostura bitters, 2 tablespoons of cola essence, and 2 tablespoons of mixed essence. Sweeten with granulated sugar to taste.

BLACK ROCK

Something new we created- a spicy infusion made with pomegranate juice, rum, dried plums and a hint of almonds. Dont't dismiss it before you try it.

200ml/7oz pomegranate juice
44ml/1½oz dark rum
44ml/1½oz white rum
3 tablespoons lemon juice
4 teaspoons amaretto syrup
2 teaspoons honey
½ teaspoon allspice
8 prunes (pitted)

1. Place the prunes into a sterile ½L/½qt/1pt Hermetic storage jar.
2. Use a blender to mix the other ingredients together.
3. Strain the liquid over the prunes.
4. Seal and refrigerate for a minimum of 24 hours. (The cocktail can be stored in this way for up to 2 months).
5. Stir the mixture with a spoon. Place 4 prunes into each mug over crushed ice and bathe with half of the liquid. Garnish with a slice of lemon and serve with a stainless steel fork.
Note: be sure to eat the prunes, they're gorgeous.

FIERY PASSION

For this cocktail, we use ready-made passionfruit juice and Rum & Red Peppers (see page 187). A spicy combination of rum, pepper, triple sec and tropical fruit juices to get you in the mood on those special occasions.

114ml/4oz passionfruit juice
28ml/1oz Rum & Red Peppers (liquid)
28ml/1oz Cointreau
14ml/½oz orange juice
14ml/½oz lime juice
7ml/¼oz grenadine
½ small red chili pepper (sliced)
1 dash Angostura bitters
(Serves 4)

Or:
8 parts passionfruit juice
4 parts Rum & Red Peppers (liquid)
4 parts Cointreau
2 parts orange juice
2 parts lime juice
1 part grenadine
Small red chili peppers (sliced, to taste)
Angostura bitters (to taste)

1. Pour the liquids into a shaker over the chili pepper and ice. Shake vigorously for 17 seconds.

2. Strain into a highball glass half filled with crushed ice.

3. Garnish with a slice of red bell pepper from the Rum & Red Peppers infusion.

4. Serve with a straw.

TRINIDADIAN SORREL

Roselle, a hibiscus plant from West Africa, has been used to create beverages for thousands of years. Known by many names, including hibiscus tea, bissap, karkadé and sorrel, it was once the favoured drink of Ancient Egyptian kings.

100g/3½oz hibiscus flower, Jamaica flower or sorrel (dried)
120g/4¼oz white sugar
3L/5¼pt/3qt water
1 cinnamon stick
1 teaspoon ginger
6 cloves
4 bay leaves (fresh or dry)
1 tablespoon rice grains

1. Pour the water into a large pan over hot heat. Add the cloves, cinnamon, ginger, bay leaves and rice (to aid fermentation) and bring to the boil for 15 minutes.
2. Add the sorrel. Cover, remove from the heat and leave to cool for an hour.
3. Strain into a suitable container. Sweeten with sugar.
For Sorrel Liqueur:
Place 1¼kg/3lbs of sorrel (dried), 1¼kg/3lbs of sugar, 750ml of white rum and 2 teaspoons of Angostura bitters into a sterilised, sealed container. Steep for one month in a cool, dark place. Strain and bottle.

CHOCOLATE RUM SHAKE

A decadently rich and creamy adult milkshake combining rum and chocolate. Share with your favourite person.

70g/2½oz chocolate ice cream
200ml/7oz whole milk
30ml/1oz dark rum
1 teaspoon honey
1 dash Angostura bitters
Garnish:
50g/1¾oz chocolate chips
(Makes 1 shake)

1. Ensure the ice cream has not melted.

2. Put everything except the chocolate chips into a blender. Blend for about 10 seconds.

3. Mix in the chocolate chips with a spoon and serve with a straw wide enough to accomodate them.

SPARTAN

Inspired by Sparta, the ancient Greek city-state of renowned military pre-eminence, our blood-red Spartan cocktail combines anise-flavoured Greek ouzo with orange-flavoured Cointreau, grenadine syrup and cherry juice.

1 part ouzo
1 part Cointreau
1 part grenadine syrup
5 parts cherry juice

1. Pour all the ingredients into a shaker with ice and shake vigorously for 17 seconds.

2. Strain into a lowball glass half filled with crushed ice.

3. Garnish with 2 maraschino cherries and serve.

PIÑA COLADA

First created in Puerto Rico during the 1950s, the piña colada or 'strained pine-apple' is very popular in the Caribbean and the Mediterranean. It has been Puerto Rico's national drink since 1978, and was made world famous after the 1979 release of 'Escape (The Piña Colada Song)', written and recorded by Rupert Holmes. In the summer heat, nothing beats a freshly made piña colada.

Wayne's Piña Colada:
6 parts pineapple juice
2 parts crushed ice
2 parts white rum
2 parts coconut milk
1 part double cream
½ part sugarcane syrup
1 pinch nutmeg
1 dash Angostura bitters

Classic Piña Colada:
170ml/6oz pineapple juice
60ml/2oz crushed ice
60ml/2oz white rum
30ml/1oz coconut cream
30ml/1oz double cream

1. Pour all the ingredients into a blender over crushed ice and pulse for 17 seconds.

2. Strain into a 12oz goblet, sling or highball glass.

3. Garnish with a pineapple wedge and/or a maraschino cherry.

4. Serve with a straw to a responsible adult.

PEPPERMINT MILO

Milo is a chocolate and malt powder that is very popular in the Caribbean and many parts of the world. Enjoy our rich, minty variation hot or cold.

300ml/10½oz whole milk
50ml/1¾oz double cream
4 tablespoons Milo
2 teaspoons peppermint extract
(Serves 2 adults or 4 children)

Hot from the hob:
Warm ingredients in a saucepan over medium heat for about 3 or 4 minutes, stirring occasionally. Do not boil. Transfer to mugs and serve.

Hot from the microwave:
Add ingredients to a small microwave jug and heat for 1-2 minutes.

Cold:
Dissolve Milo in 2 tablespoons of hot water before adding cold milk and cream. Mix ingredients and serve.

OVALTINE SUPREME

Ovaltine's distinctive flavor comes from barley malt extract and cocoa; it is also very popular in the Caribbean and many parts of the world. A hot treat.

250ml/8½oz whole milk
100ml/3½oz double cream
4 tablespoons Ovaltine
8 mini marshmallows (divided)
1 teaspoon granulated sugar
1½ teaspoons vanilla extract
(Serves 2 adults or 4 children)

Hot from the hob:
Put aside 4 marshmallows. Warm the remaining ingredients in a saucepan over medium heat for about 3 or 4 minutes, stirring occasionally. Do not boil. Get 2 large mugs. With a spoon, transfer 2 hot marshmallows per mug. Fill with Ovaltine and top each with 2 dry marshmallows. If serving 4, pour Ovaltine on one hot marshmallow per small cup, then top with 1 dry marshmallow.

Hot from the microwave:
Put aside 4 marshmallows. Add ingredients to a small microwave jug and heat for 1-2 minutes. Serve as above.

ARMENIAN STYLE COFFEE

Traditional, Armenian style coffee or sourj is brewed in a pot, without boiling. Ground coffee is mixed with water and sugar, then heated. And, it is only stirred for a second time, just before it is poured into suitable cups. This procedure extracts the most flavour from the coffee and avoids a cooked or boiled taste.

7 cups cold water (cup size: Armenian, Arabic or espresso coffee cups)
6 teaspoons Armenian, Lebanese or Turkish gound coffee
6 teaspoons granulated sugar
(Serves 6)

1. Transfer the water into an Armenian or Lebanese coffee pot and heat on moderate heat.
2. Stir in the sugar until it fully dissolves.
3. Add the coffee, one teaspoon at a time, and stir until it begins to simmer and foam rises to the top of the pot.
4. Remove the pot from the hob and reduce the heat to low.
5. Place the pot back on the hob but remove it when the foam rises again, and avoid the spillage of any coffee out of the pot.
6. Scoop out a teaspoon of foam, from the top of the pot, and deposit it at the bottom of each of your 6 coffee cups.
7. Do not allow the foam to rise again, and do not allow the coffee to boil.
8. Once brewed, stir the coffee in the pot, for the second time; then pour into your coffee cups, over the foam. Do not stir.
9. Serve with our Almond Berry Cake (see page 151), baklava or Armenian delicacies.

Note: After drinking, the coffee cups are traditionally turned over into their saucers to cool. Some believe that the patterns formed by the coffee grounds can be used for fortune telling. Nevertheless, the unique patterns can be a light-hearted source of inspiration for after-coffee conversations.

TAN

Tan is a cold, refreshing, healthy and easy to make yogurt drink from Armenia. Usually served with mint, it is an ideal summer drink, especially at barbecues.

250g/9oz plain yogurt
400ml/14oz-
500ml/17oz cold water
Salt to taste
Ice cubes
1 sprig mint (per glass)
(Serves 4-6)

1. Blend the yogurt and water in an electric blender until smooth and thoroughly mixed.

2. Add salt to taste and mix again.

3. Serve chilled with lots of ice, in a tall glass, topped with a sprig of mint.
Note: the amount of water you use would depend on whether you prefer your drink to have a thicker or thinner consistency.

DAYLIGHT SHAKE

This rich and refreshing banana milkshake will keep the young and the young at heart smiling.

70g/2½oz banana
70g/2½oz vanilla ice cream
200ml/7oz whole milk
1 teaspoon honey
½ teaspoon vanilla extract
1 dash Angostura bitters
(Makes 1 shake)

1. Ensure the banana is not overripe and the ice cream has not melted.

2. Put everything in a blender. Blend for about 10 seconds and voilà!

NOTES

NOTES

INDEX

ABOUT US

I was born in the City of San Fernando, Trinidad and Tobago, where I lived for the first 20 years of my life. My wife Sherrie is British-Armenian, born in the City of Westminster, an Inner London borough; however, she spent most of her childhood in Iraq and Lebanon with long, hot summers in Portugal. We were both blessed with mothers who were excellent cooks, born into cultures where the fine art of cooking is highly prized. In my case, I also benefitted from my mother's older sisters- all expert cooks in their own rights. Guided by my mother, and my favourite auntie, both of whom had been primary school teachers for most of their adult lives, I began experimenting with cooking from a very early age. This experience stood me in good stead when, as a young bachelor, I began studying in London. Long, international phone conversations, the exchange of family recipes and trial and error made me competent enough to cook for myself during my initial years, living on my own.

Rum & Red Peppers was conceived by Sherrie. She has a natural aptitude for cooking, which she has developed steadily, over the last 30 years. My mother shared many of her culinary secrets, but Sherrie taught herself just about everything else. And now, so many years later, I believe she is every bit as good as my mother and her sisters ever were. A dedicated, working mother herself, Sherrie has reproduced many of her most-loved, childhood dishes, adding her own distinctive flair. We live with our two talented sons, near Richmond Park, in Greater London. Together, we produced Ashes to Ashes in 1998, one of the first all-digital movies ever made and arguably Britain's first martial arts movie. And now, to celebrate 30 years of marriage, we've decided to share some of our favourite recipes, as well as several new creations, which we hope you will enjoy.

Photograph by Annie Armitage

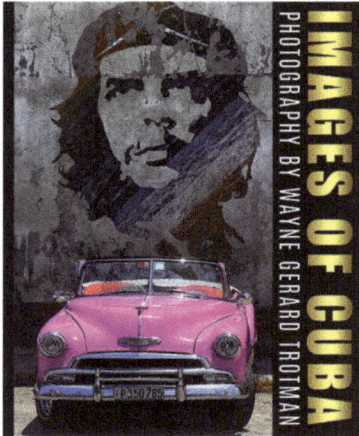

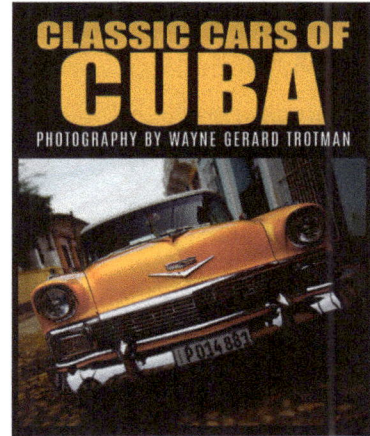

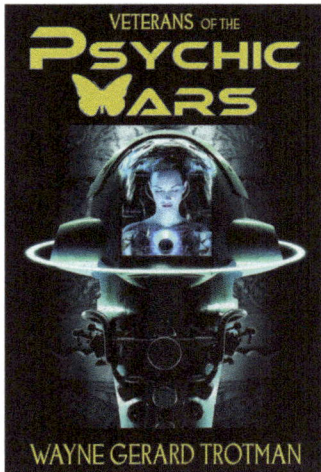

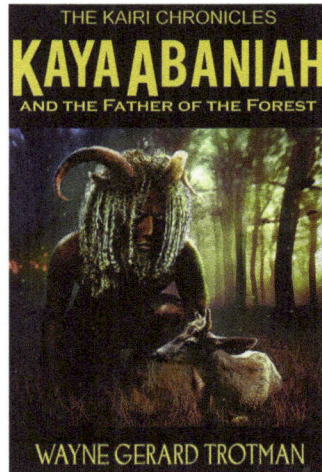

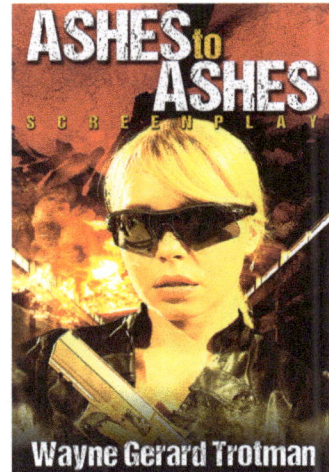